PRINCES AND PEOPLE

JOHN MILES

Princes and People

FOREWORD BY

Rt. Hon. James Griffiths, C.H., M.P.

GOMERIAN PRESS

1969

© JOHN MILES
First Impression - *May* 1969

BOOKS BY THE SAME AUTHOR

Soldiers Pocket Book — a note-book for Commando soldiers
Gerald of Wales — an essay on Giraldus Cambrensis

Printed in Wales by J. D. Lewis and Sons Ltd.
at the Gomerian Press, Llandysul

"Water and light, the earth and sky,
Is cast before you move,
And all your deeds and words,
Each truth, each lie,
Die in unjudging love".

"This Side of the Truth".
Dylan Thomas,
1914—1953.

PREFACE

THIS book is an account of some of the personalities and events that rank prominently in the astonishing history of Wales. The author is not an historian. For any mistakes he must take complete responsibility.

I am indebted to my wife for her patience, her many ideas and her striking cover design. Without her encouragement this book would never have been written. My thanks are due, too, to Harold Gresswell, of Keighley, Yorkshire, for expert advice and invaluable help in preparing the final manuscript, and to Mavis Perkins, who deciphered and typed out the first draft of the work. I owe an inestimable debt to the many writers who have so ably written on Wales, and to my friends in Wales who have given freely of their advice.

In particular I must mention Professor William Rees, who has not only helped me with his deep knowledge and kind encouragement, but, with great generosity, has allowed me to reproduce some of his maps from his *Historical Atlas of Wales*, which should be in every home.

My gratitude has been won at every stage of the writing by Mr. G. Llewellyn and the staff of the Brecon County Library, who have given me such willing help and co-operation.

My thanks are due to the Rt. Hon. James Griffiths, M.P., C.H., whose appointment as the first Secretary of State for Wales marked a climacteric in her history, for his generous Foreword.

JOHN MILES

Pytindu, Brecon
Spring, 1969.

For
RUTH
ANNE
and
CAROLYN

CONTENTS

		Page
	Introduction - - - -	15
I.	The First Prince of Wales - -	19
II.	From Earliest Times to 1066 - -	22
III.	The Norman Conquest and the Marcher Lords - - - -	32
IV.	Madoc. The Great Explorer - -	39
V.	Gerald of Wales—Giraldus Cambrensis -	47
VI.	Llywelyn the Great - - -	56
VII.	Llywelyn the Last - - -	64
VIII.	The Statute of Wales, 1284. The Edwardian Settlement - -	73
IX.	Owen Glendower - - -	76
X.	Harry of Monmouth—Henry V -	88
XI.	The Buckingham Rebellion - -	94
XII.	The First Tudor. Henry VII - -	101
XIII.	The path to Bosworth. Henry Tudor's campaign through Wales - -	113
XIV.	The Acts of Union, 1536 and 1542 -	122
XV.	Wales and the Civil Wars - -	124
XVI.	Henry Morgan—Buccaneer and Patriot -	134
XVII.	Jemima and the Black Legion The Fishguard Invasion, 1797. - -	146
XVIII.	Eisteddfodau - - - -	150
XIX.	David Lloyd George. The Welsh Wizard	154
XX.	Caravanserai - - - -	166
XXI.	The Fighting Men of Wales - -	175
XXII.	Epilogue—Wales Today - -	182
	Envoi - - - -	187

MAPS

from *The Historical Atlas of Wales* by kind permission of the Author,
Professor William Rees

	Page
Roman Wales : Roads and Forts - - -	23
Wales in 1284 : The Statute of Rhuddlan - -	74
Phases of the Glendower Revolt, 1400—1403 -	78-79
Phases of the Glendower Revolt, 1404—1409 -	80-81
Wales and the Wars of the Roses : York *v* Lancaster -	102
Henry of Richmond's march to Bosworth 1485 - -	114

FOREWORD

by Rt. Hon. James Griffiths, C.H., M.P.

WE are a nostalgic people. "Hiraeth" (longing) is deeply woven into our temperament. We love to look back and long to go back. This is why every National Festival evokes our nostalgia for all our yesterdays. When in 1969 Her Majesty Queen Elizabeth the Second presents her son Charles to our people as our Prince we shall recall the story of our Welsh Princes and the other Princes.

In this book, PRINCES AND PEOPLE, John Miles has told the story of the centuries of Welsh history. John Miles is an Englishman who came to live in our midst and who, like others who have made their home in Gwalia, has felt the magic of our story. His book is a tribute as well as a history.

Legend has it that when King Edward the First of England presented his Caernarvon born son to the Welsh chieftains he proudly claimed that this was in fulfilment of his promise that Wales should have a native born Prince who could not speak a word of English. What subsequent history reveals is that the new Prince was to be the first in a long line of Princes few of whom could speak a word of Welsh. Indeed the first investiture was to mark the beginning of attempts, reaching to the Tudor ban, to induce the Welsh people to surrender their inheritance and to forget their language.

Throughout the history related by John Miles, with its mixture of invasions and conquests, its heroism and tragedy, there runs through the story the unyielding resolve of the people to hold fast to their language. This is the greatest of all the victories related in these pages.

It is, therefore, in the fitness of things that Prince Charles should devote the months preceding his investiture as Prince of Wales to the learning of our language at the foundation College of the University of Wales. And when he is presented to the Welsh people at Caernarvon Castle he will respond in the Welsh language as well as in English. By his side will be the Secretary of State for Wales the symbol of the new status of the principality within the realm. Of all the changes in our history few have made as big an impact upon the life, and thought, of the Welsh people as those which have taken place since King George the Fifth presented his eldest son to our people half a century ago. By 1911 the Wales patterned by the first Industrial Revolution had reached the summit of its development. Our coal, slate and tinplate were in ever greater demand in the markets of the world. The people of the vales had crowded into the valleys. The ports were full of ships to carry our wealth to the ends of the world. Our prosperity seemed secure and our prospect full of promise. Within three years of that joyous event at Caernarvon Castle we were to be engulfed in the first world war and things have never been the same since. In the aftermath of war the valleys were doomed to live with poverty and frustration. Yet, despite it all our people never lost courage and have striven, and continue to strive, to build a new economy to secure the livelihood of their families and their communities. And as we acclaim our new Prince, we look forward to his joining us in our endeavour to build a new Wales within which we are resolved to ensure that our heritage will be preserved.

INTRODUCTION

It was Benjamin Disraeli, in *Contari Fleming* who said, ' Read no history but biography, for that is life without theory '. Sound advice for the general reader and also, perhaps, for the student. Certainly it goes far to justify this book, which is made up of short biographies linked and related by an account of certain events.

The author must confess that he is an Englishman, a fact which will convince many Welshmen that he was careless in the choice of his parents and in the place of his birth. He can only plead that he has done all he could since to offset these errors, and not least he has made his home on the Welsh Marches.

A book of this length can deal with only a few of the people and events that make up the story of the justly proud Principality of Wales. The choice of subjects has been made according to the degree in which the characters concerned influenced the history of the two nations.

From Pytindu can be seen Pencrug, the camp of the ancient Britons. Beyond it, on the river Usk, is the Gaer where the Spanish cavalry of the Roman Legion were stationed, and which is linked to Brecon by the Roman road. At Pytindu itself there may have been a Roman post some seven or eight hundred years before the Norman knight, Sir Richard de Peyton, was granted lands by Bernard de Neufmarche, one of William the Conqueror's barons. In the old records it is called ' The Peytevin ' and traces of the original Motte and Bailey can be seen in the grounds.

Hidden in the Groves is the Priory of St. John, now the Cathedral Church of the Diocese of Swansea and Brecon. There, too, is Ely Tower, in which was plotted the ill-fated Buckingham rebellion. Across the valley can be seen Llanddew with its beautiful church and ruins of its great castle—both associated with the colourful and courageous Gerald of Wales. In Llanddew, too, at the Standel, Rhys ap Thomas raised the red dragon of Cadwalladr on behalf of Henry Tudor, who marched to Bosworth Field where he won the English crown.

South, beyond the panorama of the Brecon Beacons, lies the

industrial belt of South Wales, that conglomeration of factories spawned by the Industrial Revolution. Dominating the town of Brecon itself is Penlan (The Headland), the recently built and ever expanding complex of schools which testify to the immense progress being made in education.

Against such a background, so inspiring and so suggestive of conflict and drama, it is hardly surprising that this book came to be written. My windows look out on to territory which is a constant reminder of the wealth of history which is to be found in Wales.

GENEALOGICAL TABLE

The table shows the descent of H.R.H. Prince Charles to the ancient House of Gwynedd

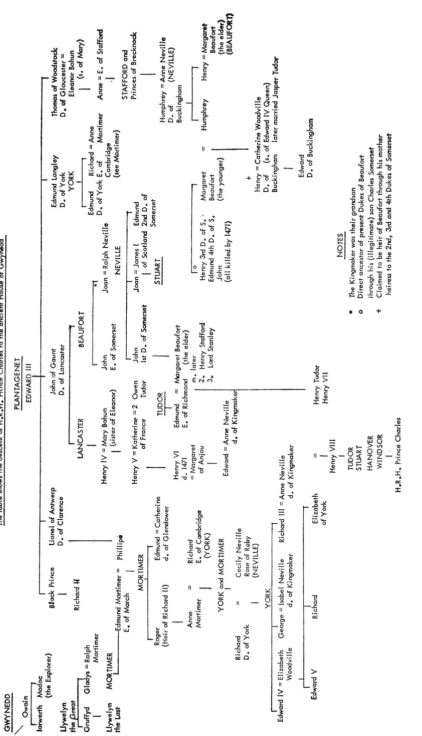

THE FIRST PRINCE OF WALES

In the spring of 1284, King Edward the First of England was making a royal progress through Wales. The fact that his wife, Eleanor of Castille, was with him, was to have no little significance. For she was in Caernarvon on the 25th of April when she gave birth to a son. This was not Edward's firstborn. There had been sons before, but they had died young. Happily, this was not to be the fate of this latest child, who was destined to become King Edward II. Unhappily, this first royal child of the dynasty of Plantagenet to be born in Wales was to prove himself utterly incompetent as a king and he was to die at the hands of a murderer when he was only forty-three.

His birth had been preceded by a bitter war between King Edward I and the native princes of Wales. Two years earlier, one of these princes, Llywelyn the Last, had lost his life in a skirmish at Irfon Bridge near Builth Wells. His brother, Dafydd, had continued the struggle against the English in the wilds of Snowdonia, but not for long. He was betrayed to his enemies and taken in chains to Shrewsbury.

In March, 1284, a special Parliament imposed on Dafydd an appalling punishment for his temerity in opposing the English. He was condemned to be drawn at the tails of horses through the streets, hanged and disembowelled and, while still alive, to be quartered and beheaded. This was the first time a political prisoner had been punished since the reign of William I, some two hundred years before. This policy of '*pour encourager les autres*' had greatly shocked the people of Wales.

In the same year King Edward I issued from Rhuddlan the Statute of Wales, the law which marked the end of independence for Wales. Thus, at the time of the birth of Prince Edward at Caernarvon the people of Wales were far from happy. The memory of Llewelyn the Last was very dear, and the manner of Dafydd's death was remembered with no little indignation. And, as ever, the people of Wales greatly cherished their independence.

King Edward, aware of the need for conciliation, decided upon a gesture of friendship. Soon after the birth of his son he summoned the Welsh chieftains into his presence. Taking the royal infant in his arms the King, it is said, presented him as their future sovereign. As he did so, he used the Welsh words, "Eich Dyn". Literally, they mean, "This is your man", but, as Edward used them, they meant, "This is your countryman and future king". In 1301 he was created Prince of Wales and Earl of Chester.

In 1346, Edward of Woodstock, better known as the Black Prince, son of Edward III and Prince of Wales, found on the battlefield of Crecy a plume of ostrich feathers and the motto ' Ich Dien '—I serve. This had been worn on the helmet of the blind King of Bohemia who had fallen fighting for the French. The Black Prince, who was sixteen years old at the time, was the real victor of the Battle of Crecy. In the fighting his father had been in command of the royal army, which had included some 5,000 Welsh archers and men at arms—at that time the corps d'elite in warfare. The Black Prince, a dutiful son, had always been popular with the people of Wales. As an act of veneration to his father and in order to show his regard for his Welsh archers, he adopted the plumes and motto of the dead Bohemian King, and ever since this has been identified with the Principality. The title is reserved for the heir to the English crown. But, on one occasion, for a few months, there were two Princes of Wales at one and the same time. This happened in 1470-71 during the Wars of the Roses, when Henry VI was enjoying his brief restoration and Edward IV had fled to self-imposed exile.

In May, 1471, Edward of Lancaster lost his life at Tewkesbury. This opened the way for Edward of York to become Prince of Wales. This was the unfortunate Edward V, the older of the two Princes in the Tower. They disappeared—most probably murdered as mere boys—in 1483, but their exact fate remains shrouded in mystery. But it was this Prince Edward of York who had the distinction of being the first Prince of Wales who could claim descent from the ancient princes of Wales.

One of his ancestors was Gladys, the daughter of Llywelyn the Great, who married Ralph Mortimer, one of the great Marcher Lords. Gladys was the ancestress of Edward IV, whose grandmother was Anne Mortimer. Through Lionel of Antwerp, Duke of Clarence, the third son of Edward III, she was the true heiress to the English throne. The throne of Richard II had been usurped by Henry Bolingbroke, Henry IV, the son of John of Gaunt, the fourth son of Edward III. This usurpation was the prime cause of the Wars of the Roses, for the Yorkists based their claim to the throne on the line of Mortimer.

When Henry Tudor assumed the throne as Henry VII and married Elizabeth, the daughter of the Yorkist Edward IV, the future Princes of Wales could claim to have in their veins the blood of Llywelyn of Wales, also known as Llywelyn the Great, as well as that of the house of Cadwalladr, from whom the Tudors sprang. Nor were these the only links the royal house had with Wales. A link that is sometimes forgotten was provided by Owen Glendower, the most romantic figure in Welsh history. It was Owen Glendower who, in 1402, married his daughter, Catherine, to Edmund Mortimer, the uncle of the aforementioned Anne Mortimer.

It is for these reasons of consanguinity that the Prince of Wales is fully justified in flying on his flag the arms of the ancient house of Gwynedd. It is for these reasons that he is the living symbol of the unity between the two nations.

It is claimed that it was a Welshman, Madoc the explorer, who, as early as 322 years before Columbus, was the first European to discover the New World. And Madoc was an uncle of the great Llywelyn, and so provides a link between our Royal House and the people of the United States of America.

FROM EARLIEST TIMES TO 1066

' Their Lord they shall praise,
Their speech they shall keep,
Their land they shall lose,
Except wild Wales '.
—A Prophecy made regarding the Ancient Britons.

BRITAIN'S position as near neighbour to the European land mass has much to do with her history. Long before the country had a navy to protect it, a succession of invaders were tempted to the island. As everyone knows, the Romans arrived in 55 B.C. But long before their advent, the island was famed for its pearls, copper, tin and gold. These valuable metals attracted those crafty, dark-skinned merchants of the East Mediterranean —the Iberians, who crossed to Britain from the peninsula which has for so long been occupied by the Spanish and Portuguese.

But Britain offered more than minerals. Its soft climate, fertile soil and abundant wild life drew land-hungry marauders from the continent. Approaching the country by way of its inviting estuaries came the Belgae, Germani and Celtae tribes which journeyed from as far afield as the Danube valley. With them they brought their skill in metal work. This was the art known as La Tene, which produced those beautiful ornaments which represent the civilization of the era.

This populating of the country was, of course, a gradual movement. And in the West and North West nature presented an obstacle to succeeding invaders of the island. There the mountains discouraged newcomers, but they also provided a refuge to those fleeing before those who had pushed their way into the country and were intent on taking over farms and village created by earlier settlers.

The first to be driven westwards were, of course, the Iberians. These were the people who, between 1860 and 1560 B.C., built Stonehenge, transporting some of the stones which form the monument from Pembrokeshire, an astonishing distance at

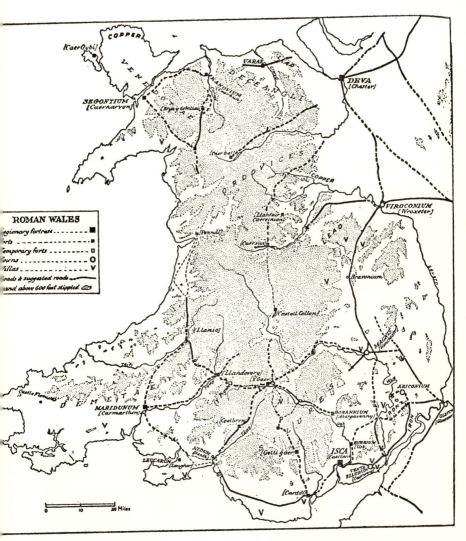

ROMAN WALES

legionary fortress .... ■
forts .... ----
temporary forts .... □
towns .... O
villas V
roads & suggested roads ---
land above 600 feet stippled

Roman Wales : Roads and Forts

from The Historical Atlas of Wales

such a period. Later, the European tribes were also to withdraw westwards, and, over the years, they intermingled with the
Iberians, the newly created race eventually becoming known as
the Celts. These were the true ancient Britons and they
provided the oldest civilization in the island.

By the time the Romans made their appearance in Britain,
the main tribes in Wales were disposed in the following manner—

The Decae Angli occupied Anglesey, which was even then
recognised as the granary of Wales, and Flint and Denbigh. The
Brythons, a highly artistic people who produced first-class
soldiers and superb horsemen, were in Montgomery and
Radnor. The Orodvices were in Merioneth and Cardigan ;
the Demetae lived in the Pembrokeshire peninsular, and the
Silures were in the territories of Monmouth and Glamorgan.

Each tribe was ruled by its own petty king and, inevitably at
that time, all the tribes were perpetually at war with each
other. Over the years the Celts had developed a clan system
bound together by ties of sentiment rather by the territorial
organisation which was beginning to develop in England.

The influence of the clan depended largely on the personality
and prowess of its leaders, whose aim was, of necessity, that of
extending the sphere of influence of the tribe at the expense of
their neighbours. It was this hostile division between the clans
which made them a too ready prey to their collective enemies.
It became the established policy of all the invaders of Britain to
exploit the mutual enmity of the tribes, playing one clan off
against another. And it was this factor which goes far to
explain why Wales never succeeded in gaining national independence.

This failure, however, was offset by a measure of success.
No invader, neither Roman nor Saxon, neither Nordic nor
Norman, ever succeeded in subduing the whole of the Principal-
ity. They had to be content with occupation of the river
valleys and the coastal plains. Wild Wales remained untamed.
This spirit of independence survives to this day. Within the
Principality the geography itself produces and does much to
preserve two nations—the North and the South.

The invasion of Britain by Julius Caesar in 55 B.C. had
little effect on Wales. It was not until close on a hundred years

later that the Romans turned their attention to Wales. They were to encounter a type of people they had not found in either Gaul or England. The tribes in these two countries had achieved a commendable degree of civilization. They preferred peace and commerce to the expensive and doubtful glories of war. They were, in the main, content to become Roman tributaries, relying on their masters for external defence.

The people of Wales did not share this supine attitude. They placed a high price on freedom and independence, and they were prepared to offer the strongest possible resistance against those who sought to subjugate them. They withstood the Romans, compelling the invaders to limit their raids to the coastal plains and penetration of the river valleys. Under Caractacus, the Silures had some success against the enemy. But, in 51 A.D., this truly great Briton was defeated near Church Stretton. He was captured and taken to Rome, where he was led in triumph through the streets. It speaks much for Caractacus that the Emperor Claudius was so impressed by the dignity of his bearing that he pardoned him for having dared to oppose the might of the Empire.

To keep order in the West the Romans established garrisons at Caerleon, where 11 Legion was stationed, and at Chester, where XX Legion was installed. In order to control the Usk valley Spanish cavalry were stationed near Brecon. Caerleon and Chester were linked by a chain of forts, but the country was never reorganised to the same extent as the territories of England. The towns the Romans did build were designed more for military than civil purposes.

The fact that they were threatened by a common foe did not unite the Welsh tribes. They continued to fight each other as well as the invader, and the Romans were quick to see that they could take advantage of this hostility between the clans. They drew into the ranks of their Legions many a tough Welshman.

In A.D. 78, that far-seeing Roman Consul, Gnaeus Julius Agricola, occupied Anglesey, the great and vital granary of the north. He had gained such a measure of success in crushing the tribes that he regarded the subjugation of Wales as complete. There were two reasons for Anglesey ranking as of such critical importance. Not only did its fat lands make its possession economically necessary, but it was also the stronghold of the influential Druids, the last remnant of the Celtic priesthood which had flourished in Europe long before the advent of the Romans. The Druidic priesthood attracted the elite. A man could be both a Druid and a leader. This meant that they made up a body which could plan and organise, and the Romans had good reason to wish to bring an end to their power. In Caesar's campaigns in Britain and in Gaul it was the Druids who had been behind every resistance movement. But, under steady pressure, they had slowly withdrawn westwards.

The Romans usually showed considerable tolerance towards religious observances in occupied territories. But they could not extend this permissiveness towards the Druids. This was a body which not only inspired and organised resistance to their rule, but which had as an integral part of their ritual the sacrifice of human beings. That is why the Romans brought such forces to bear against them that the Druids were virtually wiped out. But not entirely. In the mountains and forests—inaccessible to the invaders—the religion lingered on.

It was basic to Roman colonial policy to establish good relationships with the local inhabitants of occupied territories. In Wales this policy proved successful in some degree. Inter-marriage was encouraged, and the Legions drew into their ranks Welshmen whose warlike qualities they appreciated.

It was in the year 383, in the twilight of the Roman occu-pation, that the Emperor Magnus Maximus married the daughter of a Caernarvon chief. Welsh Princes who were to come many years later traced their descent to the issue of this marriage.

The Roman occupation lasted about 450 years. Although some Latin words were injected into it during that period, the language of Wales had remained Celtic. During the Roman rule there had been a considerable advance in culture, a worth while progress in the arts of civilization and the spread of the Christian religion. Wales, then known as Brittana Secunda—a separate state—was to wait for a long time before it was to enjoy government which had been as wise, tolerant and beneficial as the rule of the Romans. But the Romans did Wales and indeed, Britain, one grave disservice. They welcomed the fighting men of the country into their legions, but they took over the national defence. On their departure they had done nothing to provide for the vacuum their absence was bound to create. There was no competent national army, nor was there a national navy. The forces that existed were under the command of petty kings, and these rulers could rarely be persuaded to unite under one leader.

Britain lay unprotected. And this explains why the country, with the Romans no longer in occupation, stumbled into the Dark Ages, when the island suffered the depredations of a succession of invaders. Only in Wales, where the Celts—secure in their mountains—were not overrun, and where, on occasion, the people united against the invader, were the pagans repelled.

There were some leaders of insight and vision who saw that national unity was essential to the security and wellbeing of Wales. There were some who actually achieved their dream of making the people one unit. But, in every case, the system of divided inheritance—against primogeniture—made the unity impermanent. Each time a leader died, his territories were shared amongst successors and his achievements were dissipated.

During the Roman occupation, Christianity had gained a firm place in the life of the people. Spreading mainly from the West, the monastic system had established itself throughout the land. The monasteries, in fact, provided the centres around which the communities revolved. They also inspired in the Welsh that deep religious fervour—and austerity—which, for centuries, has been such a feature of their national life. It is claimed that Caractacus, who was taken to Rome and there pardoned by the Emperor, was also converted while in that city, and returned to Wales to preach the Gospel.

St. David (520—590 c), the Patron Saint of Wales whose festival is celebrated on 1st of March each year, was the son of a petty king whose domain was situated in West Wales. He not only founded the monastery of St. David's, but he also was responsible for the creation of many other monasteries and churches. Widely known for his piety and simplicity of his life, his influence was felt far beyond the confines of Wales. He earned fame in England and Ireland, and he became a legend in his lifetime. According to one story concerning St. David, he was preaching on one occasion when the ground beneath him rose so that he could dominate the congregation. At the same time, so it is said, a dove alighted on his shoulder, and this explains why he is always represented by a dove. How his name comes to be linked with leeks remains a mystery, but it has been suggested that it may have to do with the frugal manner in which he lived. A less kindly legend regarding this saint claims that he was made head of the Welsh Church because he could shout louder than any other bishop.

When the Dark Ages set in, the Christian Church remained the only national institution and influence in Wales. Pagan invaders had overrun Britain, and the Welsh felt for them such hostility that, for a long time, no attempt was made to convert these heathen neighbours. In the centuries that followed, the men of Wales accepted the struggle against the Saxons and, later, the Danes as a normal condition of life. Just as normal, they felt, were the unending feuds between the native princes and the absence of national unity, as well as the lack of a national army and a national navy.

In that 500 years of stagnation several names stand out like lighted candles in the gloom, but it is possible here to mention only a few. King Arthur is perhaps the best known of these. His court was established at Caerleon, and it is fitting that Wales should claim possession of the Holy Grail.

The Saxons became absorbed into the rest of Britain, but not so Wales. She proudly maintained her independence. And, so it was assumed, she threatened the independence of others. Which calls to memory the name of Offa, King of Mercia, who ruled his territories from Lichfield. He decided that there was such a danger from a Welsh invasion of his lands that he built a dyke which ranks as one of the most famous in the world. Offa's Dyke was a rampart of earth which stretched for a hundred miles from the mouth of the Dee to the mouth of the Wye, running along a line that was later to become known as the Welsh Marches, or boundaries. So well built was this earth-work that traces of it have survived to the present day. It formed an effective boundary between the two nations, and

King Harold saw it as so accurately setting limits to Welsh expansion that he decreed that any Welshman found East of Offa's Dyke was to suffer the penalty of losing his right hand.

Another name which commands attention is that of Rhodri the Great. Under his rule Wales made great strides towards unity. But, on his death, the country was once more divided up into autonomous kingdoms. And this division, made in 877 remained until superceded by the Edwardian Settlement.

King Alfred the Great, that most enlightened ruler, maintained peace with all the Welsh Princes. A change in the relationship took place in 885, when Alfred received their submission, in return for which he provided naval aid in her struggle aginst the Danish invaders who were harrying the coasts. That the two countries were drawing closer together is indicated by the fact that Asser, a monk of St. David's, was one of King Alfred' closest advisers.

But, as the years went by, a change of a perceptible nature was taking place in the relationship between the two nations. The English Kings were establishing a measure of supremacy. This was due to the fact that no one Welsh prince could, for long, maintain power over the whole of Wales, and so the Welsh were not in a position to protect their own coast.

In 953 Athelstan, a grandson of King Alfred, became the first real King of England. This was a united England of Saxons and Danes, which was developing, as was Normandy, along the feudal lines of Danelaw. Athelstan was a contemporary of the Welsh Prince, Howell the Good. Howell had wisely contracted a marriage which had resulted in most of Wales being united, and so he was able to treat with Athelstan on equal terms. Howell codified in writing the Welsh Law and provided Wales with its first minted coinage. But his death was the prelude to division in Wales. The inevitable civil war broke out and the chance of unity was lost once again.

His son-in-law, Llywelyn ap Seisal, restored the situation and so was able to offer resistance to the Danish marauders. He died in 1022, at a time when King Canute was ruling in England. Canute was married to Emma, the daughter of

Richard the Fearless, Duke of Normandy, a marriage that was of considerable importance to Wales. It was this marriage which brought the throne of England under Norman influence and which had its outcome in the Norman Conquest.

Emma's boy, who was Canute's stepson, was the saintly albino, Edward the Confessor. Edward had been brought up in Normandy, and he gained the throne through the efforts of Godwin, the powerful Earl of Wessex. In Harold, Godwin produced a son who proved to be exceedingly able and who became the virtual ruler of England for the childless Edward.

In Wales, too, a most capable ruler had come to the throne. This was Gruffydd, the son of Llewelyn, one of the country's greatest leaders, and whose untimely death was a disaster for the Welsh nation.

Gruffydd now became the undisputed ruler of the country. He was the bitter enemy of Harold, whom he rightly regarded as the greatest danger to a united Wales. In 1052 and again in 1055, acting on the principle that attack is the best form of defence, Gruffydd carried the war into England and, at Hereford, defeated a combined force of Saxons and Normans.

To secure an ally, Gruffydd married the daughter of Harold's greatest Saxon rival, Aelgar. For some years there was peace, and Gruffydd so extended his authority in the Principality that he was able to treat on equal terms with Edward the Confessor. Harold, a good soldier and a tireless opponent, had learned from expensive experience that the usual tactics of warfare were of no avail against the Welsh in their mountains. He took steps to correct the situation. He set about training men in mountain warfare and he also spread his agents among the Welsh chieftains.

Aelgar died, and Gruffydd lost his principal ally. The way was open for Harold to strike, and he attacked in 1062. He launched his offensive from Bristol and, with his specially trained troops, he carried the war into the Welsh mountains. Gruffydd was driven from his base in the town of Rhuddlan and he fled to the mountains which had always offered such solid refuge. But they were to prove inadequate on this occasion. Given time, there is little doubt that he could have rallied the country against his enemy. But time, although he did not know it, was the one thing he did not have. This was due to the activities of Harold's agents, who had done their work well.

Harold had offered 300 cattle for the head of Gruffydd and the reward was too much of a temptation. Gruffydd was killed by the treachery of his own men in 1063. Ironically, the chief traitor, the Bishop of Bangor, never received any part of the reward. Gruffydd was rightly mourned as the "head and shield and defender of Britain". He failed to achieve his aim, but he inspired a national spirit so strong that it has survived to this day.

Had Gruffydd lived he might have achieved the lasting peace with the Normans which was essential if Wales was to survive as an independent nation. Upon his death, however, Harold married Gruffydd's widow and placed Wales under the divided rule of Gruffydd's brothers. This, after Hastings and the death of Harold, was to prove highly expensive for the Welsh.

When William of Normandy assumed the throne of England as William the First, Wales was in much the same state in which the Romans had found it over a thousand years before. It was a loose federation of petty princes. There was no cohesive national policy or national fighting force, and it was further handicapped by a divisive system of inheritance which kept the country in an enfeebled state. She might well have achieved strength and even greatness, but to do so she needed a national army and navy based on her mountain fortresses to protect her Anglesey granary. With such an arrangement and with a strong national leader, Wales might well have remained independent, being powerful enough to come to terms with her neighbours in a manner advantageous to herself.

Until 1066, the people of Wales had not suffered as the result of foreign occupation. The tolerant Romans had governed with a light hand. With the solitary exception of Harold, the easy-going Anglo-Saxons had been content as long as the Welsh had remained on their side of Offa's Dyke. But, after Hastings, the Welsh had new and quite different neighbours. These were the restless, ruthless and supremely efficient Normans, who were determined to transform Welshmen into Englishmen.

In what measure they succeeded, and with what results, we shall see in due course.

III

THE NORMAN CONQUEST
AND THE MARCHER LORDS

' Cold heart and bloody hand
Now rule the English land '.

NORSE POET.

DURING the reign of Edward the Confessor—perhaps the only religious mystic ever to rule in England—Normans were introduced into the English court and administration. Thus, after William of Normandy became ruler, they were not strangers to the country and its ways. They came from the same stock as the previous invaders—the Danes—and there was no great difference between the two forms of government which obtained in the two countries.

Harold, for political and military reasons, had exaggerated the successes he had gained against the Welsh. His efforts to subdue them had actually achieved little, and the Normans were to find that, west of Offa's Dyke, they faced a very different and much more difficult problem from the one which had confronted them on their invasion of England. The Anglo-Saxons, a peace-loving people, were reluctant to offer much resistance to an invader, and this was particularly the case when the intruder was prepared to respect their laws and customs and offer economic advantages by opening up trade for them on the continent.

When he assumed the throne of England, William was aware of the warlike qualities of the Welsh. He also knew that their weakness lay in their inability to unite against a common enemy. Aware of this, he decided that success against them was most likely to be achieved by taking advantage of the divisions and playing one chieftain off against another.

His first task, however, was the subjugation of England and the securing of his western flank. To keep the Welsh in check during the occupation of England, the Conqueror appointed three strong barons as lords over the territories which were obvious avenues by which the Welsh might invade the regions east of Offa's Dyke. The first of these regions was Chester, pointing to the heart of Gwynedd, dominated by the great mountains of Snowdonia and approached by the narrow coastal strip. The second was Shrewsbury from which the Severn Valley penetrated into Powys, while the third was Hereford which offered a natural road into Deheubarth and the lush coastal plain of South Wales.

William created three Earldoms, one for each of these regions. Chester he placed under the corpulent, but energetic, Hugh the Wolf, also known as Hugh the Fat. Shrewsbury he gave to Roger of Montgomery, a man of considerable administrative ability, while the control of Hereford was placed in the hands of William Fitz Osbern. They were charged with the responsibility of preventing the Welsh from intruding on English soil, and they were required to make such advances as they could with their own resources. As an inducement for them to make maximum efforts to command Welsh territory, they were promised that they could hold all they managed to occupy.

When he rewarded his barons with land, the King insisted that they should govern according to the law. But these three earldoms were Counties Palatine, which meant that the earls were undisputed rulers owing no more than feudal loyalty to the King. They were allowed to administer their own justice, raise revenues according to their own determination, and make and enforce whatever laws they wished. The earls, of course, had their lesser lords, and they became known as the Lords Marcher.

It was the policy of William to transform both Normans and Saxons into Englishmen. But the Welsh were of an unbending independence of spirit. They jealously guarded their own language, customs and laws, and they had no wish to become English. So strongly did they resist domination and anglicization that almost seventy years were to elapse before South Wales was subjugated, while a further 150 years were to pass before North Wales was even in part brought to heel. At the time of the Edwardian Settlement, nearly 225 years after the Norman Conquest, the English crown had authority over only six counties. The rest of the Principality lay in the grip of the turbulent Lords Marcher who, by this time, were of mixed blood, the mixture being Norman, Welsh and Saxon.

A further 250 years were needed to settle the problems created by the rule of the Lords Marcher. And during that time nearly every rebellion against the crown had as one important ingredient the turbulent people of Wales.

The Normans made a slow penetration of the fertile valleys and the coastal plains, where they established their control, forcing the Welsh back to the untameable uplands. The advantage lay with the Normans, who had military expertise, mobility and sea power. Against the opposition of the disunited Welshmen, the efficient, ruthless and energetic Normans carried their civilization into Wales, compelling the people to accept their social and economic structure.

Geography permitted South Wales to be subjugated more rapidly than the other regions of the Principality. By 1081 King William had effectively established his authority to the extent of being able to visit St. David's. More than piety dictated this pilgrimage. The King was intent on strengthening the morale of his Norman garrisons and on making a show of his strength which would persuade the native chieftains that they would be wise to submit to his governance. In this he had some success.

King William I was able to assert his authority over his Norman barons. But by the time that his son, William Rufus, had ascended the throne (in 1087), and for many years afterwards, the Norman vassals of the border earldoms presented a far more serious threat to the English King than did the Welsh Chieftains. In fact, the Norman vassals had replaced the Welsh princelings in some measure both by conquest and intermarriage. The apparent answer to the danger then presented was for the English King to remove them, but this was not possible. They were needed to restrain the Welsh, who were always ready to strike when the opportunity presented itself.

By 1135, South and Mid Wales had been almost completely subjugated. The whole of the coastal plain and the river valleys were studded with Norman castles. Indeed, Pembroke, because of an influx of Normans, English and Flemings was known as "Little England beyond Wales". It was a centre in the Principality where the Welsh language was not used.

As the Norman advance continued it brought in its train barons, knights, men at arms, clergy and monks. It also brought architects, masons, craftsmen, merchants and farmers. All were eager to claim a stake in the occupied territories. As time passed they married with the Welsh. But the laws of inheritance did not favour the native chieftains. There were developments, however, which proved beneficial to the whole community.

Before the advent of the Normans the Welsh had led a pastoral and nomadic life. There were few towns, and geography determined the boundaries between the different districts. But, as castles were built and a much more rational and productive agricultural policy was adopted, villages were established under the shelter of the castle walls. And these eventually expanded into towns with monasteries and churches. The lords administered the district.

Some of the Welsh withdrew with their chiefs into the highlands, while others became vassals to the Normans. But the native chieftains fared so badly they were forced to supplement their needs by raids on the produce of the lush valleys.

In Wales the whole of the Middle Ages was a time of mixed and divided loyalties. The Welsh not only fought the Normans, but they also fought each other. While, as if to complement this, the Normans not only fought the Welsh, but also took up weapons against each other. It was, in fact, the Lords Marcher who really shouldered the task of subjugating Wales and not the Kings of England. In the North the task proved particularly difficult. Costly and bitter experience made the Normans aware that they could neither make any deep penetration into Welsh territory or hold what they managed to gain. The only opportunity for advance lay along the narrow, heavily forested coastal plain. The heavily armoured Normans were ready prey to the lightly armed and remarkably agile guerillas, who swooped down, struck swiftly and violently and withdrew into the inaccessible regions of Snowdonia. Earl Hugh and his immediate successors were willing to come to terms with the Welsh, but the Welsh were not prepared to come to terms with them.

The struggle in North Wales was made all the more effective because the princes there were able to achieve a degree of unity which nearly gained independence for Wales or dominion status. Many Welsh princes fought the Norman invaders, and on both sides, reflecting the spirit of the times, there was cruelty and treachery.

There are many names in the history of Wales which are worthy of remembrance. Prominent amongst these, of course, are the two Llywelyns, whose lives are dealt with in detail later.* Other names that should never be forgotten are Griffith ap Owain of Gwynedd who fought the Normans in the North, and Griffith ap Rees of Deheubarth, who not only fought the Normans at Cardigan in 1136, but also defeated them. Not to be overlooked is Owain, who twice defeated Henry II, forcing him to withdraw, and who nearly achieved the grand design of unifying Wales. Finally, there was Lord Rhys, a great warrior and statesman, who was also a lover of culture and who held his first Eisteddfod at Cardigan in 1176. Lord Rhys reached an independent arrangement with King Henry II and gave him active help in crushing a revolt of the barons.

In spite of men of this calibre and courage, the Norman influence spread and became extensive. As intermarriage became more and more common, the two races began to work together and, an inevitable development, they came to regard England as the common enemy. The Welsh tongue was preserved and Welsh common law was observed. Civil administration in Wales had been entrusted to the barons, but the first Norman Kings sought to achieve political domination through the Church in Wales. The Church remained in the hands of the Kings, who spared no effort to achieve its Normanization. Normans replaced the Welsh bishops, and the ancient ' clas ' system of the Celtic Church was destroyed. Boundaries were instituted for dioceses, archdeaconaries, rural deaneries and parishes. The bishops were required to be obedient to the Archbishop of Canterbury.

At the time that Llywelyn the Great was making his bid for the independence of Wales, Gerald of Wales was fighting for

---

*See pages 56-72.

the independence of the Welsh Church, a struggle in which he was loyally supported by the native princes. On the heels of the Norman conquerors came the various religious orders such as the Benedictines, and that reformed branch of their order, the Cluniacs. But the Cistercians were established by the Welsh chieftains, and it was the influence of this order which left the deepest and most permanent mark.

As we have seen, the Saxons offered but little resistance to the Normans. The geography of the country gave the advantage to the heavily armed forces of the invader. But in the forests and mountains of Wales, which lent themselves so exactly to guerilla tactics, the advantage lay with the Welsh. And it was not only the terrain which favoured them. It was the Welsh who invented the longbow, a weapon which was to dominate warfare for many centuries and which established itself as a decisive armament. Originally created in Monmouthshire during the reign of Henry II, in Welsh hands it could pin an armoured knight through his saddle to his horse. And the Welsh used it with deadly effect.

Edward I was the one who realized the importance of the longbow in large scale operations. He used it with Welsh mercenaries against the Scots. From then on, all the great Captains, including the Black Prince, Henry V and Edward IV, were to rely on their Welsh bowmen.

Llywelyn the Last's defiance of Edward I marked the beginning of the end of the ardently nourished hopes of Welsh independence. But, as we shall see, the settlement of 1284 left most of Wales in the hands of the Lords Marcher who, by this time, were of mixed blood and loyalties. The number of such lords was placed as high as 143, but this is probably an exaggeration. Naturally, every English monarch would have been glad to see the end of these petty, highly independent princelings. But, after 1284, when Edward I had established royal authority over the principality, every English monarch needed their co-operation in preserving what was always a highly brittle Welsh peace. Eloquent bards could always stir up trouble by recounting old injustices and the glories of past princes, and yet again the high spirited Welsh would be taking up arms. West of Offa's Dyke was recognised as a wild and lawless land where the King's writ, if it did anything, excited only contempt.

The Lords Marcher were to play a decisive part in the history of Britain. When King Edward III died suddenly in 1377 nearly all his sons were in one way or another connected with the Lords Marcher, who could command considerable support from the vassals and tenants on their vast holdings. The Wars of the Roses was a fratricidal conflict between the descendants of Edward III, and it was, basically, a struggle for power between the principal Lords Marcher.

The Lancastrian Henry Bolingbroke was Earl of Hereford due to the fact that he married a Bohun. On the other hand, the Yorkists claimed the throne through the Mortimers of Wigmore, who had been Marcher Lords since 1075 on the Shropshire border. As we have seen, they were connected by marriage to Llywelyn the Great and Owen Glendower. The Houses of York, Lancaster, Beaufort, Neville and Stafford had many links with Wales and its Marcher Lords. Finally, came Henry Tudor with Beaufort blood in his veins and a Welsh army at his back to seize the English throne.

For generations, while England prospered in comparative quiet, these Lords Marcher and the Welsh spent their lives fighting. Wales, alas, was a paradise for the mischief maker. Anyone eager to stir up trouble could slip from one lord to another or change his loyalty even more radically by going over to the native princes. But through it all Wales retained its own proud spirit and justified the description of John Milton, "An old and haughty nation, proud in Arms".

Ironically, it was the Tudor King, Henry VIII, who was responsible for Wales finally losing her long cherished independence.

IV

MADOC THE GREAT EXPLORER
1134—1170 (c)

' Madoc am I, the son of Owain Gwynedd,
With stature large and comely grace adorned,
No lands at home, nor store of wealth,
My mind was whole to search the ocean '.
—Gutyn Owen, Tr. from the Ode of Meredudd.

THE invention of printing, which so transformed the technique
of keeping records, had no impact on England until 1477. This
explains why what we know of Madoc has about it a legendary
air. It explains, too, why there remains so much uncertainty
about precise details of his life. Nevertheless, Madoc was much
more than a legend. He was very much a Welsh Prince, a man
of immense resource and courage, and an explorer who established a tradition worthy of Columbus himself. Indeed, there is
strong evidence that, in 1170, well over 300 years before
Columbus arrived in America, Madoc the Welshman reached
the shores of the New World. What is more, there is good
reason to believe that he founded a colony there—at Mobile
Bay, Alabama, on the Gulf of Mexico—where there is a memorial of his great achievements.

Since the beginning of man there have been travellers' tales of
unknown lands situated on the other side of the Western Ocean
—far beyond the Pillars of Hercules,* which marked the
western extremity of the ancient world. Plato (c. 427—348
B.C.), Aristotle (384—322 B.C.), and Seneca (c. 4 B.C.—
A.D. 65), all made reference to this distant and unknown land.
It was, of course, the Phoenicians who originally peopled Wales,
and, in the year 100 B.C. it was claimed that the same people
had extended their explorations much further afield. In fact, it
was said that they had discovered a "Large, sweet, fertile island

---

*Two promontories, Calpe (Gibraltar) in Europe and Abyla (Ceuta)
in Africa.

opposite to Africa". There appears to be a blank of several hundred years before any further attempt was made to visit these faraway territories. But in the 6th century A.D., St. Brandon, who earned himself the title of the Irish Ulysses, sailed the western seas for seven years during his search for the Isle of the Saints. Tales were told from generation to generation about his discovery of new lands.

Perhaps it was these tales which inspired the Vikings, Erik the Red and his son, Leif, to venture far out into the western waters. In any case, during the tenth and eleventh centuries these two made voyages which convinced them that there was a landmass on the other side of the Atlantic Ocean. Thus, by the twelfth century, although little was known about it, what was to become known as the New World was much more than folklore and legend. It was widely accepted as a reality, offering a challenge to anyone who had the courage and skill to venture out on the wide waters. It promised land to those who possessed none. Just such a man was Madoc of the princely house of Gwynedd in North Wales.

In 1138, Owain succeeded his father as Prince of Gwynedd. Through his father he was closely connected with the Scandinavian Kings of Dublin. Owain is remembered as a great King. Deservedly, he is equally well remembered for his exceptional virility. He had two wives and, after the fashion of Solomon, several concubines, and by these women he had, so tradition claims, some 27 sons. Madoc was one of these, but his mother was merely one of Owain's mistresses, and so he was illegitimate. Nevertheless, he was not only the son of a great King, but also of Brenda, the daughter of the Lord of Carno.

The date of his birth is uncertain, but it is thought he was born sometimes between 1134 and 1142, and that he came into the world at Dolwyddelan Castle in North Wales. With so many sons, there must have been doubt and dispute as to the succession, and it is said that, in order to ensure that there was no further contender for the title, Owain ordered that his son should be slain at birth. But luckily for Madoc, he was smuggled away by his mother, and it may be that he spent his years of exile in Ireland.

As a child, he was known for his skill in the making and handling of boats. He studied the coracles and curraghs, which were composed of wicker frames covered with skins, and he watched the larger plank ships being built. No doubt, like the young Raleigh and Henry Morgan, he listened to the many stirring tales of the Vikings and of the voyages of St. Brandon told to him by his Irish-Scandinavian kinsmen. From them he learnt of lands awaiting the impress of the foot of the explorer.

His grandfather was a great lover of music and famed as a patron of minstrels, and it was in the guise of one of these that, at the age of sixteen, he returned to his father's court. The disguise must have been a good one, as his father failed to recognise him. Not so his mother. She knew him, and took him in her arms. It was at this unlucky moment than Owain came upon them. Not surprisingly, a man of such a virile nature, drew the wrong conclusion, and Madoc was again driven into exile. Some time later father and son were reconciled, and Madoc took his place at his father's court. He also married, his wife being Annesta, a maid of honour to one of his father's wives.

It was now that he began to earn his reputation as a sailor. Within three years he travelled widely, visiting Ireland, Conrwall and Brittany. In 1163 he represented his father as an emissary to the Lord of Lundy, whose support Owain sought in his struggle against Henry II. This was a period when a change was taking place in travel by sea. The coracles and curraghs in which men had ventured on the waters for so many hundreds of years were giving place to the tough, tubby plank ships which were equipped with square sails. These vessels had a straight keel with a stern rudder and were capable of carrying from twenty to thirty men. Navigation was still a hazardous business, the way being made by the sun by day and the stars by night. The compass in use was inevitably very elementary, being no more than a needle magnetized by a lodestone floating in a bowl of water. Madoc had considerable knowledge of navigation and seamanship, and he owed this to the Vikings. As for his understanding of astronomy, he owed that, as did so many others, to the druids of Anglesey. He was well fitted for a man of his time to undertake long voyages. But, of course, he

was ill-equipped to face the hazards and uncertainties of unknown waters compared with that other royal explorer, Prince
Henry of Portugal, known as Henry the Navigator. But this
grandson of John of Gaunt did not appear for another three
centuries, by which time the techniques of sailing had been
considerably improved.

In 1169 the great Owain died, having ruled for nearly
thirty-two years. During his lifetime he had not only given to
Wales some twenty-seven sons, but he had also furnished the
country with a considerable degree of unity and a distinct Welsh
culture. But, on his death, what he had foreseen and feared,
happened. Dissention broke out over the succession, with the
result that North Wales was plunged into the miseries of a civil
war. These events proved of decisive significance for Madoc.
They made him realise that there was no place for him in his
native lands. Even if there had been, it is doubtful whether he
would have remained. For his mind had for long been respond-
ing to the call of the sea and of the unknown. And so, with his
brother Rhryd, who had the title of Lord of Clochran, and who
shared his love of the sea, and his brother Einion, who was
subject to the lure of the unknown, he discussed the possibilities
of venturing upon the great waters. During his stay in Lundy,
in 1163, he had given no little thought to the excitements and
satisfactions he was likely to find in such an enterprise. Now
circumstances compelled him to set forth. He needed new
lands where he might begin a new life.

His first voyage was made in the company of Einion,
Rhryd did not go with them. He had inherited lands in Ireland,
and he felt that they called for his attention. It is difficult to
say how many vessels were involved, but it seems that not more
than three ships made the journey, and there might have been
only two. Whatever the number, they included Madoc's
flagship, the *Gwennon Garn*. Those which set forth had been
built under Madoc's personal supervision. Made of wood from
the forest of Nant Gwynant in Caernarvonshire, the records say
that stag horns were used to secure the planks instead of nails.
This, in fact, was a normal Viking practice. As a safety
measure the hulls may have been covered, as were coracles,
with cow hide tanned on oak bark. The ships were built at

Abergele on the border between Denbighshire and Caernarvonshire.

It is impossible to say just when the expedition set out, but the available evidence indicates that it was sometime in 1170. The point of departure was Aber Kenion Gwnyon, now known as Rhos-on-Sea, near Colwyn Bay. Madoc and Einion made their way by a south west course, leaving Ireland to the North. They passed east of the Azores and the ships, carried by the current, made the crossing of the Atlantic, finding landfall at Mobile Bay on the Gulf of Mexico. Madoc was delighted by what he saw. He said that he had found a land, "affording health, aire, gold, good water and plenty of nature's blessings". The last must be taken to mean that the land was fertile.

From the very beginning the voyage had been regarded as no more than a reconnaissance. It seems reasonable to assume that Madoc had promised to return to Wales for Rhryd, who could command much larger resources for the founding of a colony. Having settled his company, Madoc recrossed the Atlantic, and the account he was able to give of what he had found on the other side of the ocean aroused such enthusiasm that a much larger expedition was organised. Obviously with a view to giving the colony permanence, women were included in this undertaking. The pioneers set out from Lundy, Rhryd in a ship named *Pedr Sant*. But none of the ships ever returned and no one—at least, no Welshman—ever saw any of the members of the expedition again.

Nevertheless, there is sufficient evidence to show that the vessels were not engulfed by the Atlantic. That the expedition set out is proved by a stone found on Lundy island some years ago. Engraved in lettering in the old Welsh style, it is in Latin, and the translation reads : "It is an established fact known far and wide, that Madoc ventured far out into the Western Ocean never to return". And the story of Madoc was handed down and became almost an Arthurian legend among the people of Wales. That it was received with credence in high places cannot be doubted. When Henry Tudor came to the throne in 1485 as Henry VII, he gave orders that a searching enquiry should be made into the matter.

Much more than idle curiosity prompted this action. Since the days of Madoc there had been considerable advances in the arts of navigation, and there had been improvements, too, both in boat building and map making. All these developments had combined to increase knowledge of the New World. It was now regarded as a reality. Henry, like many of his contemporaries, saw in these lands believed to exist beyond the western waters a new and much needed outlet for the energies that were being released by the Renaissance.

This, of course, was the age of Christopher Columbus. He was much more than a superb sailor. He was a man with a keen eye to business. His quest was not only for new worlds, it was also for larger wealth. His interest in the little known territories beyond the Atlantic must have caused him to enquire in every way open to him into the expeditions which had taken men to their mysterious destinations. As a business man he realised that he would need sponsors for the kind of undertaking he had in mind, and he knew that any sponsor would want adequate reassurance that he had a reasonable chance of making a worth while return on his money. He would need to show that others had crossed the great ocean before him, coming upon rich and promising lands.

Henry VII's interest in Madoc was as practical as was that of Columbus. During the second half of the fifteenth century, due to the shrewd acumen of the merchant Prince, King Edward IV, England had developed an economy that ranked as one of the most prosperous in Europe. London had established herself as the centre of world trade, and her ships and seamen visited many countries. This great commercial advance had been achieved against the distrubed background provoked by the Wars of the Roses. But the Battle of Bosworth, which ended those wars and which brought the first of the Tudors to the English throne did not blunt the will to expand. If anything, it sharpened this profitable determination. Henry VII, in fact, was a most competent business man. So true was this that it was to Henry that Columbus sent his first prospectus regarding an expedition to the New World. It was the brother of Columbus, Bartolome, who brought details of the proposed voyage to the English court. And it is certain that he made mention of Madoc. As for Henry, he was so interested in the proposal that he instructed Bartolome to return to Columbus and request him to come to London, bringing with him his detailed plans and charts.

But for a piece of sheer misfortune, it might have been England who sponsored Columbus's historic journey across the Atlantic. But on his way home, Bartolome fell into the hands of pirates, and when he eventually reached Spain his brother had already set sail. But it was none other than Christopher Columbus who provided the most reliable evidence to support the claim that Madoc had crossed the Atlantic before him. On his return from his first voyage he told of a people who honoured the memory of a man called Matec. And on his chart, near the Gulf of Mexico, was written most significantly, "These are Welsh waters". Further proof of Madoc's presence on the shores of the New World is provided by the Spaniards. For many years in Nova Hispana, (Florida) as the new land was first known, they tried to seek out the "gente blanco" who had first arrived at the land they themselves claimed to have discovered.

No attempt is being made to extol Madoc above Christopher Columbus. Indeed, nothing can detract from the magnificent achievements of the one who is credited with discovering America and returning to Europe to announce a find that was to raise the standard of living for the world to unprecedented heights. His achievement might be likened to that of the first man to land on the moon, which will be the prelude to space exploration. But the contribution made by others to the achievements of Columbus cannot be overlooked. St. Brandon, Erik the Red and Leif, as well as the Carmelite priest, Nicholas of Lyne, all played their part. But none made a greater contribution than Madoc of Wales. That Madoc made his astonishing crossings of the Atlantic is supported by the highest possible testimony. Amongst those who made reference to Madoc are Hernando Cortez, who captured Mexico for Spain, Sir Walter Raleigh, Sir John Hawkins and the colourful Montezuma II, King of Mexico.

Cortez spoke of America being peopled by a strange race from far across the sea. This might appeal as being vague, but Sir

Walter Raleigh was much more specific. He told of Welsh words used by the Indians. While Sir John Hawkins reported that the Mexican chiefs believed they were descended from the ancient Brythons who came from the land of the rising sun. As for Montezuma, when he made a treaty with the Spaniards, he stated that his people came from a little island in the north.

Over the centuries the tradition of Madoc had been accepted, and it would seem that he was, indeed, one of the world's greatest explorers and pioneers. Certainly it has by the Virginian Cavalier Chapter of the Daughters of the American Revolution. At Fort Morgan, in Mobile Bay, Alabama, they have set up a fitting memorial to the uncle of Prince Llywelyn the Great and ancestor of H.R.H. Princes Charles. It reads :

' In memory of Prince Madoc, a Welsh explorer,
who landed on the shores of Mobile Bay in 1170 and
left behind, with the Indians, the Welsh language '.

Thus on Lundy, the point of his departure, and at Mobile Bay, the point of his arrival, there are memorials to Madoc the Explorer. But, alas, it seems that little is known of him in Wales. As far as I know, in all the country there is not one monument to this amazing man. He is, alas, a prophet who has failed to find honour in his own country.

V

GERALD OF WALES

GIRALDUS CAMBRENSIS
1147—1223

' I am sprung from the princes of Wales and from the barons of the Marches, and when I see injustice in either race, I hate it '.
—Giraldus.

FRUSTRATION! That one word might well have served as the epitaph of Gerald of Wales. He was destined to fail and to go on failing, although, all the evidence suggests, he had everything in his favour.

He devoted his life to achieving two supreme ambitions—that of becoming head of the see of St. David's and that of securing the independence of the Welsh Church. Throughout the reign of three kings he deployed all his great gifts and his many advantages to achieve these aims. And all to no purpose. The Welsh Church was to achieve its independence, but not until almost 700 years after his death.

Had he been content to become merely a bishop, then he would have been amply satisfied. He was offered numerous bishoprics in Ireland, and he was invited to accept the sees of Bangor and Llandaff. But his heart was set on St. David's, and that alone could satisfy him. It was a see that was always to be denied him. As for an independent Welsh Church, that was still a dream that was far indeed from fulfilment on the day he expired.

Gerald was born at Manorbier Castle, near Tenby, in 1147, and he could hardly have had a more promising beginning. His noble birth was in itself in immense advantage, as patronage in those days played a large part in preferment. His father was a Norman noble, William de Barri, a man of considerable wealth. On his mother's side, Gerald could trace his ancestry back to the first Princes of Wales. In addition, he had connections with the leading families of both Wales and Ireland.

Blessed with good looks, an acute intelligence and quick wit, he also had the benefit of boundless energy. Offsetting these qualities, as all the evidence suggests, was his pride which can only be described as inordinate.

His father's brother, David Fitzgerald, was the Lord Bishop of St. David's, and it was this uncle who was to be responsible for Gerald's education. He could hardly have had a more suitable mentor. It was the influence of David Fitzgerald which resulted in Gerald deciding on an ecclesiastical career. And it was during these impressionable years that he developed his lifelong love of St. David's and of the Welsh Church. He continued his education at Gloucester, afterwards spending three years in Paris, where he studied rhetoric and theology. He has left it on record, a typical testimony to his pride, that in Paris "the really model scholar was Gerald the Welshman".

Returning to Wales in 1172, he was ordained as a priest. Two years before, the struggle between King Henry II and Thomas à Beckett had culminated in the assassination of the Archbishop, an act which had produced a profound effect on Gerald. It served to strengthen his dedication to the church. Due to the patronage of his uncle, as well as to his own remarkable gifts, he quickly gained promotion. And his energy and intelligence soon established him as a person of no little merit amongst both the clergy and laity. He did not spare himself in his efforts to increase respect for the church. His uncle, although a scholar and devout, had shown himself to be a lax administrator. The diocese was in poor shape, with the discipline of the clergy at a low level. Gerald was not content to administer the diocese. He also ruled it. He was young and no more than a priest, but any attempt to usurp ecclesiastical obligations aroused his fierce resistance, no matter how exalted the offender might be.

The Archdeaconry of Brecon was in the lewd hands of an ecclesiastic named Jourdain. But it could not remain so when Gerald took command in the diocese. Jourdain, although an Archdeacon, had been living in concubinage in Llanddew for years, and his influence had been the opposite of what it should have been. Gerald removed the Archdeacon from his benefice. He himself was appointed to the office, which he occupied for over twenty-five years, making Llanddew his principal residence in the diocese.

Bishop David died in 1176, and almost everyone assumed that Gerald was bound to be his successor. It seemed both right and natural that the man who had administered the diocese for so many years should assume his uncle's mitre. The Chapter forwarded its nomination to the King, and it was merely courtesy which caused them to include the names of the other three archdeacons in the diocese. After all, one name would have seemed like a command to the monarch, and it never occurred to anyone that Henry II would refuse to ratify the appointment. So sure was everyone of this that, without awaiting the royal approval, the nomination of Gerald was acclaimed throughout the diocese and Te Deums were sung in many of the churches.

This, far from having Henry's approval, excited his anger. The Chapter had taken his consent for granted and in this, so he claimed, they had insulted him. But that was a minor matter. Politically, Gerald was unacceptable to the King. Wales was still a turbulent country, only too prone to rebellion. Gerald, a descendant of the Royal House of Wales, and with so many influential connections, might well become a serious problem if endowed with the authority of a Bishop.

Henry refused to so much as consider Gerald for the vacancy, appointing in his stead the Cluniac Prior of Wenlock, Peter de Leia. As angry as he was disappointed, Gerald went to Paris, where he remained until 1180, when he became reconciled to the King. On returning to Wales he was formally appointed Commissary of the Diocese of St. David's. But he was, in fact, Bishop in all but name, as Peter de Leia had shown himself quite unequal to the responsibilities of the office.

Well aware of Gerald's many qualities, the King, in 1185, made him a Royal Chaplain, and when Prince John was appointed to rule Ireland, Gerald went with him. While touring the country, he was offered, and refused, two Irish Bishoprics. Perhaps because he did not like John, he was soon back in his beloved St. David's, once more playing a prominent part in the running of the diocese. At this time he was on excellent terms with the clergy, the court and with Baldwin, the

Archbishop of Canterbury. In 1188, in fact, he accompanied the Archbishop on a tour of Wales, preaching the Third Crusade. It was on this crusade, in 1190, that Archbishop Baldwin died, and Gerald was sent to Wales to keep the peace on behalf of the King. Again he was offered two bishoprics, this time those of Bangor and Llandaff, but refused both. In 1192, he retired to Lincoln to study and pursue his writing, a course he was prompted to adopt because he feared the vacant see of Canterbury would go to his old enemy, Hubert Walter. This, in fact, is what happened. And it was Walter who used his influence to prevent him becoming Bishop of St. David's when his chance came again. This happened in 1198, when Bishop de Leia died, and when Archbishop Walter was virtually ruler of the country. The Chapter were as much aware of Walter's hostility as was Gerald. Nevertheless, they made him their first choice, adding to their list, as custom required, three other names. But the Archbishop proposed to the King, that the new bishop should be Geoffrey Henlaw, Prior of Llanthony and a Doctor of Medicine. Gerald, no doubt greatly affronted, said that the Prior had the Archbishop's support because his pills had helped the Prelate recover from an illness.

The Chapter of St. David's, anxious to see Gerald receive the appointment, decided to make a personal representation to King Richard. But when the delegation bearing the plea that Gerald should be given preferment arrived in Normandy it was to find that the King was dead. They also learnt that Richard had nominated his younger brother, John, and not his nephew, Prince Arthur, as his successor.

The new King was crowned at Westminster in May, 1199, and showed himself gracious towards the Chapter—at first. Indeed, he gave the impression that he was quite willing to accept the nomination of Gerald to the see of St. David's. So sure were they of this that Gerald rode off to the diocese, where he was received in triumph by clergy and people. The Chapter elected him to the See, confident that he must be made Bishop. But even while this was happening, Archbishop Walter was persuading the King to veto the appointment. Gerald, unaware that John had changed his mind, was sure that his life's dream was about to become a reality. He decided that this was an

opportune moment to strike a blow that would mean independence for the Welsh church. He would receive his consecration
from the hands of the Pope, himself. But already his hopes were
being deferred. Even while the people of the diocese of St.
David's were rejoicing and celebrating Gerald's preferment, a
peremptory order was received by the Chapter nominating
Geoffrey Henlaw to the vacant see.

The Chapter protested, and Gerald decided to go to Rome,
there to plead his case with the Pope. The occupant of the
papal throne was none other than Innocent III, one of the
greatest of the papal fathers. Gerald was received courteously,
and he reminded His Holiness that, until the time of the first
Henry (who reigned from 1100—1135) the Welsh Church
had been subject only to Rome. He also made the most of this
opportunity to reveal his wit and depth of his learning, and he
told stories which revealed errors in Archbishop Walter's
theology and scholarship.

But Gerald was not the only one who was busy. So, too, was
the Archbishop of Canterbury. Knowing that Gerald was in
Rome and that he would be supporting his pleas with offers of
large tithes from Wales, Walter, too, made bids for the papal
favour, and they were much larger than anything Gerald had to
offer. And the Archbishop was exercising his influence in
Wales, and to some purpose. In Wales, due to his inspiration, a
strong party was created to oppose Gerald and to further the
cause of the Abbot of St. Dogmaels

The struggle dragged on, with no decision being reached, and
it was proving a serious drain on Gerald's resources. But the
bishopric meant too much to him for him to surrender it without
every effort being made to secure it. In 1201 he set out for
Rome once more, although by this time another name had
been put forward for the vacant office. This latest nominee was
the Englishman, Reginald Foliat, blandly dismissed by Gerald
as unsuitable because he was unversed in the Welsh tongue.

Innocent III appointed a commission to enquire into the
matter, and although the see of St. David's had been without a
bishop for three years, the hearing was adjourned until All
Saints' Day (Nov. 1st) the following year. This further post-
ponement of a decision must have been a severe disappointment

to Gerald, but worse awaited him when he returned to Wales. On reaching home he found that he had lost the support of the Chapter. Having lost official backing, he still refused to admit his cause was lost. He turned for help to the people of Wales and received offers of help from powerful relatives. It seemed that there might be an attempt to force the issue by a resort to open rebellion. Gerald was declared an outlaw and a rebel.

Whether the Papal Commission would have decided in favour of Gerald had he shown himself less intractable no one can say. But when it finally issued its findings, it announced that it found in Foliat their choice for the bishopric. Even this blow failed to daunt Gerald. He lost no time in excommunicating Foliat and also Osbert, the Archdeacon of Carmarthen. Then he hurried off to Rome, taking with him letters of commendation from the Welsh Princes. Foliat and Osbert were also in Rome. In spite of this, Gerald's mission was not a complete failure. Although he did not persuade the Pope to nominate him to the vacant office, Innocent was so affected by his argument that he annulled the election of Foliat and directed the Chapter of St. David's to make further nominations.

By this time, Gerald had exhausted his resources and contracted a heavy burden of debt. Unable to stay longer in Rome, he made what proved to be a dangerous journey across Europe, learning on the way that the Archbishop of Canterbury—apparently as indefatigable as himself—had procured yet another nomination and that the matter was being decided at Rouen. Gerald lost no time in visiting Rouen, where he denounced the aims of Archbishop Walter, and then resumed his journey home. On arriving in Wales, he found the Archdeaconry in disorder, and even more discouraging was the discovery that the supporters of his idea of an independent Welsh Church had dwindled to two—one old lady in addition to himself !

Yet a further writ was issued. The Chapter of St. David's met at Waltham, but their deliberations ended in a failure to agree. They met again, this time at Lambeth, but with no better result.

The struggle had by this time spanned five years, and, for Gerald, they had been five very expensive years. And now, he was without either money or supporters. It was at this point that Fitz Peter, the Judiciary, advised him that he should accept the fact that the forces arrayed against him were not to be defeated ; that he would be wise to accept the inescapable truth that he was not to be allowed to become Bishop of St. David's. But it was not only for his own sake that he should accept the inevitable, but also for the sake of the Church and for the diocese he loved. In making his plea, Fitz Peter was able to produce some highly persuasive arguments. Gerald would be wise to relinquish his hopes and give his support to an honest Englishman rather than have the office conferred upon a Welsh candidate who had so treacherously betrayed and deceived him. There was, too, the cowardice and disloyalty of those for whom Gerald had fought. Finally, there had been what appeared to be the mercenary attitude of the Papal Court, influenced in their attitude more by the money they would gain from the appointment than by the quality of the man who was to occupy the bishopric.

The climax was reached in the Chapel of St. Catherine in Westminster Abbey on May 10th, 1203. Gerald knew that it was the intention of the Chapter to nominate Geoffrey Henlaw, Prior of Llanthony, who was a member of the Chapter of St. David's. Gerald had no personal quarrel with this man, and, to the surprise and delight of all present, he signified that he was willing to have Henlaw consecrated as Bishop of the diocese. The struggle, which had lasted five bitter years, was over. That Gerald had given all he had in the struggle, meeting every fresh blow and disappointment with undiminished resolution, was a truth to which the Prince of Powys bore witness when he said : "Many a great war have we Welshmen waged against England, but none so great and fierce as his who fought the King and Archbishop and withstood the might of the whole clergy and people of England for the honour of Wales".

Geoffrey Henlaw was made Bishop of St. David's. Peace was restored between Gerald, the King and Archbishop. He was awarded a pension and reimbursed for all that his suit had cost him. But he decided to sever his connection with the diocese of St. David's which, he judged rightly, had treated him in an unforgivable manner. He resigned the Archdeaconry of Brecon and set out on a pilgrimage to Rome. He was received with honour and made a Brother of the English College there known as the Hospital of the Holy Spirit.

Gerald has left it on record that he came very near to being offered the red hat of a cardinal, and it seems that there was some substance in this. For the Pope had reason to be grateful to him. The Pope had appointed Stephen Langton to succeed Hubert Walter as Archbishop of Canterbury, and King John had shown no liking for the choice. The dispute over the election had precipitated the King's unsuccessful quarrel with the Church. John had tried to embroil Gerald in the dispute, but the Welshman had refused to support the royal cause. He liked Langton and had no faith in John. It may well be that his attitude in this matter had caused his name to be mentioned in connection with a Cardinalate.

Unfortunately for him, he was never to be offered the bishopric he so greatly coveted. In fact, in this connection he was to suffer yet another disappointment. This happened in 1214, when Geoffrey Henlaw died, and St. David's was again a vacant see. Gerald took no part in the nomination and election of Henlaw's successor, but his writings reveal that he was offended when he was passed over in favour of Iorwerth, Abbot of Talley.

Gerald of Wales died in 1223 at Manorbier, where a memorial was raised to him. He was buried in the precincts of the lovely Cathedral of St. David's, and his statue stands in the Trinity Chapel in the Cathedral. He is depicted as a scholar but, by a neat touch, the sculptor drew attention to his failure to achieve his cherished aim by placing a mitre at Gerald's feet. There can be little doubt that it is his failure, with all its ironic overtones, that adds interest to his life. He was one of the most colourful personalities Wales has given to history, and the pulpit in the small parish church of St. David, Llanddew, near Brecon, is a fitting tribute to his character and qualities.

Today, Gerald is chiefly remembered for his writings, being best known as a topographer. His *Topgraphia Hibernia* recounts his journey through Ireland in the company of Prince John, and his *Itineriarium Kambriae* records his journey through Wales during Archbishop Baldwin's crusade. But he wrote on a wide range of subjects, including history and natural history, geography, canon law, divinity and, inevitably in view of his nature, biography. He was also famed as a first-class raconteur and writer of letters and, in common with so many of his countrymen, he was a poet.

His critics claim that he was too credulous as a scholar and far too vain, and it must be admitted that he was far from faultless. But he was a man of many parts, a great patriot and a great personality. It is indeed as a highly gifted human being, rather than as a saint, that he earns his place in history.

It was on 31st March, 1920, almost seven centuries after has death, that his other dream—that of an independent Church in Wales—was realised. By an Act of Parliament the Welsh Church became disestablished and a Welsh Archbishopric was formed. The church in Wales ceased to be a part of the province of Canterbury. It became free to decide its own policies and administration. This act of acquiring freedom for the Welsh Church would have rejoiced the heart of Gerald of Wales.

VI

LLYWELYN THE GREAT
1173—1240

'His country's strongest shield'.—Dafydd Benfras.

In 1136 there took place the Battle of Cardigan, in which the Welsh forces were victorious over an army of Norman barons. By this time, chastened by some fifty years of experience, the Welsh had mastered much of the Norman arts of warfare. But there was a harder lesson they had failed to learn. They had not yet realised that national unity was essential if Wales was not to remain outside the orbit of the English kingdom. And it was, inevitably, the policy of the English Kings to bring Wales under their jurisdiction.

It was Owain Gwynedd, a soldier, statesman and man of action, who saw that Welsh independence called for Welsh national unity. By force of his personality he persuaded many of the native chieftains to work in association with him. He also made alliances with the princely House of Dynevor, from whom came the paramount chieftains of Wales. But these efforts were brought to nought due to the treachery of Owain's brother.

Henry II came to the throne in 1154, and it was one of his avowed purposes to subjugate Wales and to unite it firmly with England. Owain faced an enemy whose resources were much greater than his own. Even so, for a time he proved to be a match for his adversaries. In North Wales geography favoured the defenders. The invaders faced mountainous country known intimately to the Welsh and fully exploited in the struggle against the English. Owain, for some time, had reason to be satisfied with the way the struggle was shaping. Henry II marched from Chester, reached Rhuddlan and occupied Anglesey, but he was unable to hold his gains. He withdrew and, three years later, he made a further attempt to overwhelm Welsh opposition. But, in 1157 he was no more successful than in 1154. Twelve years later, he made a third attempt, this time using Oswestry as his starting point. Owain awaited his enemy who was leading the might of England and a most powerful national army. The two forces met at Corwen, and what the outcome might have been had not the weather intervened can hardly be in doubt. But savage rains and wind wrecked the English purpose and Henry was compelled to retire once again.

Thus Owain managed to preserve the independence of his country. He was praised by Gerald of Wales as a wise and moderate ruler. But, whilst all the Welsh chieftains held him in respect, they were utterly opposed to surrendering the least degree of their own individual and divisive power. Thus unity remained a precarious and readily lost shield, requiring all the time a dominating personality in order to maintain it. Luckily for Wales, when Owain died, they found just the man they needed in Lord Rhys. He had those rare and great qualities which won respect and affection and so he was able to preserve the unity Owain had achieved. Lord Rhys, too, had the breadth of vision and political insight which enabled him to turn an enemy into a friend. He did this with Henry II, who by this time was heavily committed in Ireland and who was having no little domestic trouble with his barons. Rhys lent Henry support in crushing the revolt of the English lords. In this way he won the respect and gratitude of the English King and there was peace between the two nations.

Lord Rhys displayed in large measure that love of culture and learning for which the Welsh have for so long been famous. It was under the patronage of Lord Rhys that the tradition of the Eisteddfod was established in Cardigan in 1176. But this progressive and rational outlook was not shared by all the people of Wales, with the result that the external peace protecting the country was not matched by the same degree of internal peace. Owain had been the father of many sons and, on his death, they quarrelled bitterly, striving to determine by force who should possess and exercise power. It was only to Madoc that Wales owed anything. But, in 1173, in Dolwyddelan, North Wales, a grandson was born to Owain. This was Llywelyn ap Iorwerth, destined to achieve fame and to earn the title of Llywelyn the Great. To him Wales came to owe a great deal.

Llywelyn had a claim to the territory of Gwynedd through his grandfather, Owain, and he also had a claim on the region of Powys through his great-grandfather. But hereditary rights were less decisive in determining who actually entered into possession of land and property than were a strong arm, courage and personality. Happily for Llywelyn, he was richly endowed with these qualities.

He also had other advantages. He had been supplanted while still very young by his uncle, Dafydd the First, and he had spent many of his more formative years in England where he received a good education and learnt to understand and appreciate the qualities of the English.

Pursuing the policy initiated by Lord Rhys, Dafydd had allied himself with Henry II. He had also, in 1188, entertained Archbishop Baldwin and Gerald of Wales at Rhuddlan when they were preaching the Third Crusade. Whether the effort and expense of the crusade were to Dafydd's liking is uncertain, but it was a matter which claimed little of Llywelyn's attention. During his years of exile in England, he had kept in touch with events in Wales and, in 1194, he decided that an opportune moment had arrived for his return. His uncle was overthrown, and Llywelyn seized a power he had always regarded as his by right.

This man was not only a skilful politician, but he was also a realist. During the early years of his reign he gave almost the whole of his time and energies to the complicated purpose of making his throne secure. He did this by effecting alliances with the Welsh chieftains. His main difficulties were created by his own family and in overcoming the problems involved in achieving satisfactory relationships with the powerful princes of Powys. For some eight years he pursued this primary purpose of uniting the Welsh people and, by 1202, he had the satisfaction of knowing that he had succeeded. He was recognised both in the North and South as the leader and spokesman of Wales.

He was, above all, a patriot and he was greatly concerned that his country should be safe against external aggression. A statesman with a rare breadth of vision, he saw clearly that it would be wise to come to terms with neighbouring England. It was obvious that to attempt to settle differences with a neighbour blessed with significantly larger resources by other than peaceful means could only prove costly, if not disastrous, to Wales. He decided that his country should be associated with England in a form of dominion status. In those days this was a perfectly normal and acceptable arrangement, and it meant that Llywelyn was required to acknowledge the overlordship of the English crown on behalf of the Welsh nation. But it did not call for any loss of independence in self-government on the part of Wales. It was an arrangement that promised to be beneficial to both sides. And it certainly met Llywelyn's aims, which were, of course, the advancement of Welsh interests and the promotion of Welsh prestige.

If Llywelyn sought self-aggrandisement, this found no expression in his claiming for himself, as did his grandson, the title of Prince of Wales. He was too much a realist not to understand that the Welsh would only rarely and always reluctantly submit to the rule of a fellow Welshman. Prince was a title he eschewed. But he saw that nothing could be lost and that much might be gained by cementing and fostering friendship with England. That is why he married Joan, the daughter of King John, in 1206. Joan, it was true, was an illegitimate offspring of the English King, but this did not invalidate her worth as the monarch's daughter. Bastardy in those days lacked the ill repute it has acquired since. In any case, Joan was later recognised as legitimate by her step-brother, Henry III.

Unfortunately for Llywelyn, things were not to develop in the way that his diplomacy and insight deserved. It is true that, in the years immediately following upon his marriage to Joan, he was able to consolidate his position and further his aim of creating a united Wales. But the Welsh chieftains remained a divisive element in the nation, nursing for each other a dangerous degree of hostility and suspicion. This was a weakness in the Welsh position which by no means escaped the notice of the crafty, power-loving King John, who was curiously and inaptly named "Lackland".* As a Marcher Lord, he knew a great

---

*Name given as he was the youngest son with no territorial inheritance.

deal about Wales, and he aimed at subverting the kingdom by playing off the Welsh chieftains one against the other.

By 1208, the relationship between England and Wales was anything but friendly. And, in the twelve months that followed, Llywelyn and King John were in open opposition, a situation that was by no means to Llywelyn's liking. In an effort to avoid outright hostilities between the two peoples, he sent his wife, Joan, to make an offer of submission to her father. But "Lackland's" aim was not submission. It was subjugation. And, in 1212, he was making determined efforts to achieve this end. But this threat to their national independence only served to unite the people and chieftains of Wales under the leadership of Llywelyn. He achieved a high degree of unity, and so much so that he was able to convene a representative Council of Wales. This was made up of chieftains and leading citizens and it was held at Aberdovey.

Although he knew he had Wales fully united against a common enemy, Llywelyn pursued his aim of strengthening his country's defences against a most powerful and cunning enemy. To secure himself against the English Crown, he contracted marriage alliances for his children with members of the powerful families of the Lords Marcher. The first husband of his daughter, Gladys, was Reginald de Broes, Lord of Brecknock, and when he died, she married Ralph Mortimer of Wigmore. This union has considerable historical significance, as it is through this alliance that the British royal family trace their descent from Llywelyn the Great.

It can be said of Llywelyn that he made the Welsh nation, a fact which was recognised by Pope Innocent III. At that time the English King was quarrelling with the Pope, for John had a penchant for making enemies and causing conflict. And it occurred to the papacy that it would displease King John if the Welsh princes were absolved from feudal allegiance to the English crown. Innocent III lost no time in promulgating this absolution. But this was a matter which claimed little of the English King's attention, for by now he was embroiled in domestic troubles which were to prove his undoing. And Llywelyn was shrewd enough to take full advantage of "Lackland's" preoccupation.

In the Magna Carta of 1215 Wales was recognised as a separate kingdom. According to its terms, Welshmen were to have restored to them their lost lands and liberties. More important, it was laid down that disputes between Welshmen were to be settled in Wales by Welsh law, while disputes in the Marches were to be decided by Marcher Law. This was a great step forward.

King John was overthrown by the barons and died at Newark in 1216. But before this happened Llywelyn was recognised as the Prince of all the regions of Wales not held by the Lords Marcher, and he accepted the title of Prince of Aberffraw and Lord of Snowdon.

King John was succeeded by his young son, Henry III, Joan's step-brother. But the power behind the throne was the shrewd and exceedingly able William Marshall, Earl of Pembroke. The barons in compelling King John to sign Magna Carta and in deposing him had set a limit to the power of the throne. But they had also increased their own authority, and Marshall embarked on a policy of reducing their power. Amongst those whom he regarded as having a dangerous ascendancy was, of course, Llywelyn, and efforts were made to bring him and his kingdom into subjection to the English crown. This resulted in intermittent fighting in Wales during the next few years as well as on the Marches. Both the Welsh and English forces achieved a measure of success, but the fighting proved inconclusive. In 1234 this state of affairs was brought to an end by the signing of the Pact of Middle. This established a peace which was to last the rest of Llywelyn's life.

Llywelyn was very much alive to the dangers inherent in the Welsh system of inheritance, which resulted in power and property being divided amongst several heirs. He saw that if his life's work was to be given permanence then the Welsh must accept the rule of primogeniture, by which the eldest son retained the power which had been possessed by the father. He was also anxious that his successor should continue the policy he had pursued of preserving understanding with the English. This, of course, was bound up with the one who would succeed him as his heir. His eldest son, Gruffydd, was illegitimate, but this by no means debarred him from being granted the succession.

The decision, however, as to who was to take over after the death of Llywelyn lay in the hands of Llywelyn himself, and he might well have named Gruffydd as his heir. But this firstborn had always opposed the policy of accepting the English King as the feudal overlord of Wales. In fact, he was leader of the war party which favoured the complete separation of the two nations. Because of this, in 1229, Llywelyn nominated as his successor his son Dafydd, who, in contrast with his illegitimate half-brother, was peace loving and moderate in his views. He had something else which was very much in his favour, as far as Llywelyn's plans were concerned. He was a nephew of Henry III. The nomination of Dafydd as Llywelyn's heir was accepted by Henry III, who, at the time, was in need of help in an expedition against the French.

It is not surprising that the people of Wales, and least of all Gruffydd, were far from happy in Llywelyn's choice of heir, and it was only because of his remarkable strength of personality that he was able to pursue his policies. In 1237 he made a formal submission to Henry III, but in doing so he sacrificed none of Wales's highly valued independence. Wales lost none of the power to govern herself. The ceremony pledging allegiance committed both nations to pursuing a policy of peace and of mutual aid against a common enemy. This was an achievement of the greatest importance, and it crowned Llywelyn's life work.

He was, however, concerned with other kingdoms beside those of this world, and when his wife, Joan, died he turned his attention to the church, seeking spiritual strength and comfort in the Cistercian brotherhood of Strata Florida. In 1238 he summoned his last Council and handed over power to his son, Dafydd.

Prince Llywelyn deserves his title of "The Great". He earned it because of his courage, his generosity of heart and mind and his remarkably keen political foresight. The Welsh owed him a great deal. He established civil administration in the country, and he built up a powerful feudal state which he associated on peaceful terms with England without sacrificing so much as one degree of national sovereignty. He was alive to the value of the arts, and he gave every encouragement to the spread of literature, poetry and music. Despite his embroilment in politics and warfare, he was of a devout disposition, and he gave his full support to the Church.

He died at Aberconway in 1240, already a Welsh immortal. His epitaph was most fittingly written by Professor T. F. Tout : "He was certainly the greatest of the native rulers of Wales . . . If other Welsh Kings were equally warlike, the son of Iorwerth was by far the most politic of them . . . While never forgetting his position as champion of the Welsh race, he used with consummate skill the differences and rivalries of the English. Under him the Welsh race, language and tradition began a new lease of life".

VII

LLYWELYN THE LAST
1230(c)—1282

'Valiant Llywelyn, the bravest of Welshmen,
A man who loved not to slink
In the easiest way out '.
> —Bleddyn Fardd, *Tr.* D. M. Lloyd.

IN common with almost all truly great men, when Llywelyn ap Ioreth died, he left a vacuum which no one else could fill. In all Wales there was no one who possessed his rare qualities of statesmanship. He had nominated as his successor his younger son, Dafydd, who was also a nephew of Henry III. In 1238, while his father was still alive, Dafydd had received the fealty of all the lesser princes of Wales. The following year he showed himself capable of treachery. By means of a trick, he made his elder brother, Gruffydd, a prisoner, and it was in this wretched state that Gruffydd lived until his death.

This incarceration, although unjust, at least ensured that, on the death of Llywelyn the Great, Dafydd was able to enter into his inheritance without Wales being torn by fratricidal strife. But this man, who could now regard himself as head of the Welsh nation, was woefully lacking in the qualities his father had possessed in such large measure. He was also childless, and this, along with his inherent limitations of character and imagination, created a potentially dangerous situation.

In May, 1240, he gave evidence of his intention to continue his father's policy towards England when he made an act of submission to Henry III at Gloucester. But there was a dispute between the King and Dafydd regarding certain territories, and the disagreement dragged on for some months. It was finally resolved in 1241, when the King compelled Dafydd to surrender all claims to these territories and also to transfer his brother into the royal keeping. And so Gruffydd exchanged the prison in which he had been confined by his brother for the inhospitable precincts of the Tower of London.

LLYWELYN THE LAST 65

Henry, feeling that he was in a weak position vis-à-vis the Welsh, decided that he needed Gruffydd as a hostage to ensure Dafydd did not indulge in any acts of aggression.

Gruffydd, however, possessed some of the courage and determination shown by his father, and he made a bid to escape from the Tower in 1244. It was an act which cost him his life. The death of his brother so incensed Dafydd that he at once took up arms against Henry, and he pursued his campaign with such enterprise and skill that, for a time, he outgeneralled the King's forces. For two years he continued to make war against the English, and hostilities had reached no conclusion when, in 1236, he unexpectedly died. He left no children and, inevitably, the structure built with such care and foresight by Llywelyn the Great collapsed.

In the death of Dafydd a measure of posthumous justice was done to his brother. For, although Dafydd had no children, Gruffydd had two sons, the younger Llywelyn who was fated to become known as Llywelyn the Last. He had enjoyed the favour of his Uncle Dafydd and was probably regarded as heir rather than was his elder brother, known as Owain the Red.

There were, however, others who felt entitled to stake a claim to Dafydd's inheritance. Llywelyn the Great, in addition to his sons, had a daughter. This was Gladys, who was married to the powerful Marcher Lord, Ralph Mortimer. Because of this relationship, Mortimer claimed that he was entitled to the succession. But none other than the King of England claimed that he, too, was entitled to a decisive say in the matter. He maintained that his son, Prince Edward, who later came to the English throne as Edward I, was the one who should step into Dafydd's shoes. He had the right to do this, Henry III asserted, because Senena, the wife of Gruffydd, had made such an agreement. It was this doubtful claim which may well explain the bitter hostility that was to exist between Llywelyn and Prince Edward. It may be that it was these claims by Mortimer and Henry which caused Llywelyn and Owain to share the inheritance. In doing this, instead of fighting each other, they united and continued the struggle against the English.

It seems that they prosecuted their war against England to such effect that both Mortimer and Henry dropped their claims to the Welsh inheritance and, in 1247, the Peace of Woodstock was signed in which the brothers were recognised as the rightful heirs of the territories of Wales But, as a condition of King Henry accepting the treaty, they had to surrender all land east of the River Conway to the English Crown They had also to do homage to Henry.

Nevertheless, by their sacrifice they had secured peace between themselves and England, and this was seen as an advantage to both countries But the lack of a common enemy created a new danger The brothers became more and more estranged until, in 1255, they quarelled and so the precarious unity of Wales was lost once more. Fortunately for Llywelyn, the English King was heavily engaged with quarrelsome barons and with rebellious Lords Marcher, and so was in no position to intervene in Welsh affairs He was also fortunate in the situation within Wales, where the chieftains were so divided amongst themselves that he was able to make himself master of the nation By 1258, most of the Welsh princes had declared their allegiance to him rather than to the English King, and Llywelyn was in such a powerful position that he declared himself Prince of Wales.

Nine years later, Llywelyn had so cemented his position that Henry III recognised his right to the title in the Treaty of Montgomery. Under this treaty only the Prince of Wales paid fealty to the English crown. The Welsh chieftains paid homage to Llywelyn. But this arrangement was by no means acceptable to the Welsh chieftains. They were incensed that Llywelyn had assumed the title. As Llewelyn the Great had foreseen, the Welsh would not submit to rule being invested in one of themselves.

Throughout this period Henry III was having ample troubles of his own. His brother-in-law, the powerful Norman-English earl, Simon de Montfort, that great champion of the people's rights had led a revolt in which at Lewes in 1264, he had made the King his captive. De Montfort had compelled Henry to accept a parliament made up, not only of barons knights and church leaders, but also of two citizens from every borough in England. This was seen by the King as an affront of the first magnitude and it was one for which Llywelyn was partly responsible. For the Welsh Prince had done more than act as an ally of Simon de Montfort. He had not hesitated to become betrothed to de Montfort's daughter, Eleanor. But this proved to be but a short step on a long journey to matrimony, as Edward I was able to hold de Montfort's daughter in detention at Windsor as a guarantee that Llywelyn would behave in accordance with Edward's wishes.

In 1265 Simon de Montfort was killed at Evesham and this marked the end of Henry's troubles with his barons. This also changed the position vis-à-vis Llywelyn, who was now proving to be his own worst enemy. He was beginning to lose the support of the Lords Marcher and also that of his own country-men. His weakness was his excessive arrogance, which so readily alienated sympathy. Nevertheless, his decline had not yet begun. He concluded the Treaty of Montgomery which marked the height of his career. Although in this he agreed to pay tribute to the English Crown, it was a statesmanlike document and indicated that he was by no means lacking in political insight.

In 1272 Prince Edward succeeded his father coming to the throne as Edward I. Before this, Henry III had left the conduct of Welsh affairs to Edward, and, no doubt, this had not given Llywelyn much cause to like or even respect the new King, who was to gain a place in history as the ' Hammer of the Scots '. He was to prove himself equally efficient at hammering the Welsh. Edward, in fact, was one of the great scions of the House of Plantagenet. Although Llywelyn had shown no small degree of wisdom in dealing with Henry III, he showed a woeful and disastrous lack of political sense in his dealings with Edward. As if bent on offending the new King, he failed to pay tribute, thus setting aside the Treaty of Montgomery. He added insult to this injury by declining to make an oath of submission to the new monarch. He was invited to attend the coronation, but he did not do so. This was the slight which so enraged Edward I that he decided to retain Eleanor de Montfort as a hostage and so frustrate Llywelyn and try to ensure his good behaviour.

It so happened, however, that things were not going well for Llywelyn in Wales. His brother Dafydd had risen in revolt against him and, along with other rebels, he had fled to England. This state of affairs did not induce the Prince of Wales to deal diplomatically with Edward. Five times, he was summoned to appear before the English King and five times, on the flimsiest of pretexts, he declined the invitations. He made it known to Edward that he would not appear at the English court as long as Edward was harbouring Dafydd and his associates, nor would he be seen there as long as his bride was denied her freedom.

Even the meekest of monarchs would have received these refusals—in view of the treaty obligations Llywelyn had freely contracted at Montgomery—as studied and gratuitous insults. But Edward I was by no means meek, and they were taken as tantamount to acts of aggression. They were largely responsible for Wales ultimately losing her independence. But things might not have reached that abysmal level had Llywelyn not indulged yet another act of provocation. He sent a list of his grievances to the Pope and claimed that it was Edward who was refusing to honour the obligations imposed by the Treaty.

There were, as in all such quarrels, grievances on both sides, but there can be no doubt that it was Llywelyn who proved the more intransigent of the two and who must take the major blame in the quarrel. It seems that he had become blind to new realities. He acted towards Edward I as if he were as indifferent a ruler as Henry III. He failed to take into account the significant fact that the baronial wars were over. But his most serious miscalculations concerned his own position in Wales. He failed to see that he had no significant support in his own country nor on the Welsh border.

In 1277 hostilities broke out. What Llywelyn had been unable or unwilling to see until now, he could ignore no longer. As soon as Edward I began operations, Llywelyn's vassals rebelled. Against most inadequate opposition, Edward marched into the heart of North Wales and, having secured the passes, he pressed on into Snowdonia. At the same time his forces were busy at sea. His fleet from the Cinque Ports ravaged Anglesey and cut off Llywelyn's communications and supplies. Edward was exploiting in the most advantageous manner his sea power. Llywelyn, deserted by those on whom he had blindly depended, heavily outnumbered by his enemies and unable to secure the instruments of war, was compelled to submit. On November 9th, 1277 he admitted that he was defeated and placed what could only have been his reluctant signature to the Treaty of Conway. This stripped him of all his possessions with the exception of a part of Gwynedd and the Isle of Anglesey. It left him still Prince of Wales, but it was a title which had lost all meaning.

Edward now had no reason to continue detaining Eleanor de Montfort. She was released, and Llywelyn married her in the presence of King Edward himself and his Queen, as well as the King of Scotland, at Worcester Cathedral. It will be recalled that Simon de Montfort had married the sister of Henry III, an alliance which meant that King Edward and Llywelyn's bride were cousins. It might have been imagined that this relationship would have reconciled the Welsh people to the overlordship of the English crown. But, as so often happened in Welsh history, an event had the opposite effect to that which might logically have been expected. The action of the English army and also the English administrators in the Principality served to inflame the spirit of national unity and purpose. Dafydd, apparently as much affected as all other Welshmen by these developments, became reconciled to his brother.

Bitter experience had taught Llywelyn at least one lesson. He now saw the wisdom of honouring treaty obligations. He also had in Eleanor a wife who acted as an intermediary between himself and King Edward. Because of this an uneasy and dangerously brittle peace existed—for a time. But the two men found themselves in deep disagreement. The main source of their difference concerned certain territories to which they both laid claim. These disputes provoked acrimonious debate as to who should decide to whom the lands in question belonged. Llywelyn argued that, since certain lands had lain within the Principality before 1277, when the Treaty of Conway had been signed, then their ownership should be tried according to Welsh law and custom. Edward not only disagreed with this line of reasoning, but he also resisted Llywelyn's claims concerning the boundaries Realising that the matters were not to be tried by Welsh law, Llywelyn demanded that they should be settled according to Marcher law. Edward responded to this by blandly decreeing, on patently inadequate evidence, that the lands were in England—that is, that they were in that part of the Principality administered by the Crown. He also informed Llywelyn that the dispute would be decided at a place of his choosing.

Even this kind of provocation might not have erupted in rebellion on the part of the people of Wales, but they were incensed by the severity with which the Principality was being administered. The Welsh were seething with discontent, but it was not Llywelyn who resorted to arms. It was his brother, Dafydd who, on Palm Sunday, 1282, stormed and captured Hawarden Castle. This, inevitably, provoked a strong reaction. But it was no isolated incident. The attack on Harwarden Castle seemed to be a signal for which the Welsh had been waiting. Simultaneously, insurrection broke out throughout the country, and it must be assumed that this was no accident, but the adoption of a well prepared plan. In such a situation both Llywelyn and King Edward were forced to take action. Llywelyn, whether he wished to do so or not, had no choice but to throw in his lot with the rebels. Edward was compelled to treat the Welsh uprising as an act of war.

The two rivals now faced each other in mortal combat. The rebels enjoyed some initial successes, taking the castles of Flint and Rhuddlan. But Edward was far from idle. He marched into Wales, but it seems that he was far from certain of the outcome of an outright war with the Principality. Even at this late stage he was prepared to treat with Llywelyn, and through Peckham, the Archbishop of Canterbury, he made a generous offer. Perhaps, had he been free to do so, Llywelyn would have acaepted the terms for a settlement, but he was forced to reject them in order to placate his Welsh allies.

Five years before King Edward had starved Llywelyn into surrender in Snowdonia, but there was to be no such outcome to the present engagement. Having shown magnanimity, Edward set his heart on settling the Welsh problem once and for all. And in this purpose luck was to favour him. Encouraged by his successes, Llywelyn made his way south to unite his forces with those of Mortimer and to gain support in that part of Wales. On the 11th December, 1282, at Irfon Bridge, near Builth

Wells, he had the misfortune to be separated from his men. He was attacked and struck down by a party of troops under Stephen de Francton, who was unaware of the identity of his victim.

It has been prophesied that Llywelyn would wear his crown in London. The King saw to it that the prophecy was fulfilled in a savagely ironical manner. Llywelyn's head was taken to London and, fixed on a pole at the Tower, was displayed mockingly crowned with a chaplet of ivy. His princely crown was placed at the shrine of Edward the Confessor in Westminster Abbey. Dafydd, who had died in 1246, had possessed the regalia of the Princes of Wales, which included the Crown Jewels of King Arthur and, so it was claimed, a piece of the Truw Cross. These were all confiscated on Llywelyn's death. And the Principality suffered considerable humiliation. This latest battle between the two nations caused Edward to take steps to ensure that there should be no further trouble from the Welsh. In 1284 he produced the Statute of Wales which spelled the end of Welsh independence.

It is fair to describe Llywelyn the Last as a magnificent failure. His ambitions were larger than those of his grandfather, but his statesmanship was not of the same high order. He was unable to translate his dreams into reality because, due to defects in his own character, he was unable to gain the affection and confidence of his fellow princes. It might also be said that he was a victim of misfortune. He was not responsible for the assault on Harwarden which sparked off the final conflict with Edward. The geography of his country was against him, as were the divisive system of inheritance, the lack of political unity, the absence of a national army and the lack of a Welsh fleet. Had he not died at Builth Wells he might have found it possible to restore his position and come to terms with Edward. Only when it was too late was he beginning to understand the nature of the English King.

Llywelyn's most serious blunder was made ten years before he lost his life—on the accession of Edward I. Had he then accepted the King of England as feudal overlord it might well have transpired that Wales, like Scotland, would have retained a large degree of independence throughout the crucial reign of

Edward I. Had this happened, the Principality would have remained a sovereign state throughout the Middle Ages. Had this been the position, it was one which Owen Glendower would have exploited to the full.

Llywelyn the Last, inspired by his dreams of independence, was undoubtedly a great Welshman. He was brave, generous, stubborn and impulsive, embodying the Welsh passion for freedom. In fact, he will always be remembered as the symbol of Welsh independence. His memorial is to be seen at Cilmeri, near Builth Wells.

VIII

THE EDWARDIAN SETTLEMENT
1284

IN 1284, King Edward I, known as the English Justinian,* drew up the Statute of Wales, which is sometimes called the Statute of Rhuddlan. This was not an enactment. It was a codification of his policy towards Wales.

It had always been the aim of all the Norman and Plantaganet Kings to extend the area over which the Crown and English administration operated. There had been a continuous effort to apply to the Welsh the criminal law and legal procedure that obtained in England. The crown, except as overlord, exercised no control over those regions of Wales which were in the hands of the Lords Marcher.

The Statute of Wales did not try to interfere in Welsh affairs to any great extent. On the contrary, it laid it down that Welsh Common Law, language and customs would be respected. It sought to dispossess no one of their lands, but allowed them to retain their holdings, provided only that they made peace with the King. It did not even seek to put an end to "gavelkind", the damaging Welsh system of divided inheritance, but it did add the provision that illegitimate sons could not be successors, that lawful widows were to be entitled to a dower, and that women could succeed when there was no male heir.

The Settlement also dealt with the counties of Caernarvon, Anglesey, Merioneth, Flint, Cardigan and Carmarthen, which were to become shires on the English model. Pembroke was to continue as a County Palatine, owing direct allegiance to the crown, with Glamorgan as an independent lordship. The rest of Wales was to remain in the hands of Lords Marcher. In order to hold Wales, or to "civilize it", royal castles were built at Conway, Caernarvon, Harlech, Criccieth and Bere, with royal boroughs standing in the shadow of their walls. These were

---

*Justinian I, the Eastern Roman emperor, reorganised and codified Roman Law.

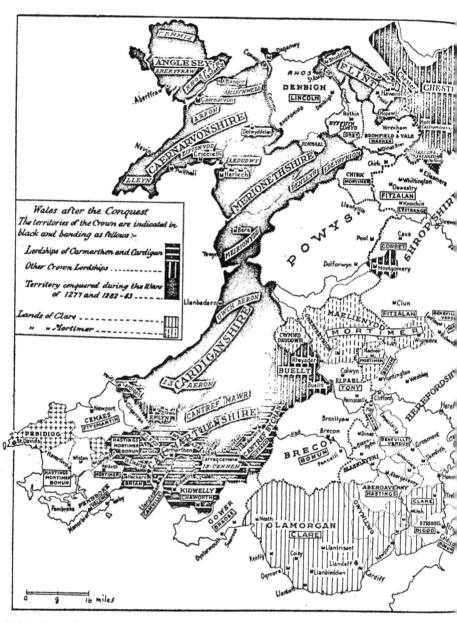

Wales in 1284 : The Statute of Rhuddlan   *from The Historical Atlas of Wal.*

quite different from the baronial castles and boroughs which had sprung up in the Marches of Wales. The royal boroughs were, in fact, nothing less than English colonies with interests that linked them with the castles. In these boroughs the Welsh were not allowed to live, nor were they allowed to hold property in them.

Taken as a whole, the Edwardian Settlement, which was drawn up more than 200 years after the Conquest, was by no means unreasonable, and it showed a much more generous spirit than did the Act of Union drawn up by Henry VIII well over two hundred years later.

Comparison is sometimes made beteeen Wales and Scotland, as it is felt that the latter enjoys a larger measure of independence. If this is so, the reason is to be found in the two centuries that followed on the Norman Conquest. Study of the period reveals why Wales, though under English rule more completely and for a longer period than Scotland, is today more Celtic in character and language. In the 200 years following upon the Conquest, Scotland absorbed Norman language and adopted Norman institutions.* Thus when Edward I set out to conquer Scotland he was making war on another feudal nation. But in Wales, since 1066, the English had been resisted as rapacious invaders, bent on changing the language and tribal customs of a loose federation of princes who were not always united amongst themselves. In Wales no separate national Parliamentary system ever really evolved, leaving a void which, not unnaturally, the Normans never filled.

---

*Except in the Highlands which still retain the Gaelic and clan loyalty.

IX

OWEN GLENDOWER
1354(c)—1416

> ' *at my nativity*
> *the font of heaven was full of fiery shapes*
> *of burning crossets : and at my birth*
> *the frame and huge foundation of this earth*
> *shaked like a coward.*'
>
> SHAKESPEARE, *Henry IV*, Part I.

AMIDST all the great Welshmen—and their number is large—Owain Glyndwr stands supreme. In him the spirit and romance of Wales found its most perfect expression. So great and numerous were his qualities that he became a legend in his lifetime, an achievement which is very rare indeed. Mystery surrounds his birth, his death and his burial, so giving to his story all the allure of an Arthurian romance.

When he was born no one knows for certain, but it is believed that it was about the year 1354. But where he was born remains to this day a matter of conjecture and debate. There is reason to believe that he first drew breath in Sycharth in Denbigh. There are those who insist that he was born in Trefynan near Haverfordwest. And there are others who maintain that his birthplace was none other than Glyndyfrydwy by Llangollen.

Wherever he first saw the light, he came from an illustrious line. Through his father he was descended from the last princes of Powys. On his mother's side he was of the ancient royal house of Deheubarth. In 1378 he came into the heritage of the Llywelyns, which entitled him to display the lions passant of Gwynedd.

His education was of a high standard. Having spent some years at Oxford, he later went to London where he studied law at the Temple. He acquired the social graces in no less a place than the luxurious court of Richard II. Although he was to prove himself so accurately a representative Welshman, he

was so proud of his English education that Shakespeare had him
say :
> ' I can speak English, Lord, as well as you :
> For I was trained up in the English Court '.

A musician of considerable talent, he has the distinction in this
sphere of introducing the harp to the English Court.

He distinguished himself, however, in whatever field he had
cause to enter. Militarily, he was to prove himself repeatedly
and under the most difficult and, at times, discouraging circumstances. He learned his soldiering in the Scottish campaign of
1385, where he proved himself a master in the arts of war. The
bards have made abiding records of his exploits at Berwick
where, wearing a scarlet flamingo feather in his helmet, he
drove the Scots before him headlong like wild goats. In 1387 he
again proved himself in battle when he fought at Radcot Bridge
as an esquire to Henry Bolingbroke. But there was to be irony
in the relationship of the two men. For it was as Henry IV
that Bolingbroke was to be Glendower's enemy and who was to
fight him over the years.

During the reign of Richard II he spent some time at Court
and then he retired to his estates and beautiful home on the
banks of the river Dee where, all accounts agree, he was most
happy in his family life. His wife was Margaret, the daughter of
David Hanmer of Maelor, a Judge of the King's Bench, and
they had what has been described as "a brood of little Princes".
In fact, they had six sons. But they also had "a brood of little
Princesses", for they also had several daughters, although just
how many is not known.

Glendower was always loyal to Richard II. In fact, he
accompanied his King on the journey to Ireland in 1399 which
was to have such an unfortunate outcome for the monarch. He
left the royal party at Flint on the way home, and he never saw
Richard again. For the King was deposed and imprisoned by
Glendower's former comrade, Henry Bolingbroke, who
assumed the crown as Henry IV.

It is difficult to discover just what Glendower felt about this
change of monarchs, but the scant evidence there is suggests
that he was not unduly perturbed by the new accession. By 1400
Richard was dead, and Glendower was pursuing the type of life

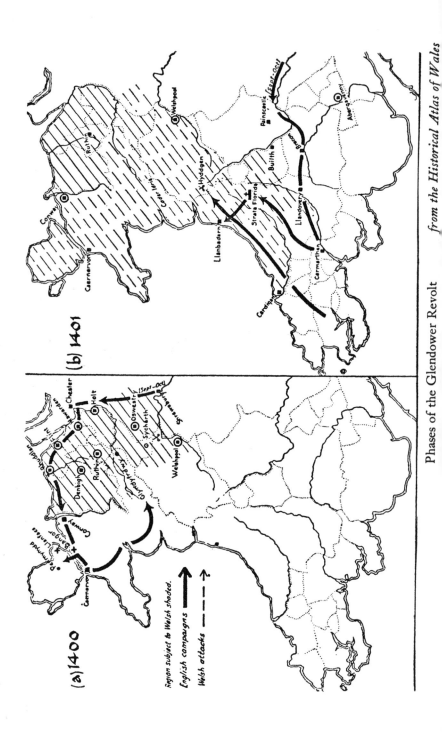

(a) 1400

(b) 1401

Region subject to Welsh shaded.
English campaigns →
Welsh attacks ⇢

Phases of the Glendower Revolt   from the Historical Atlas of Wales

(a) 1400: Caernarvon, Penmynydd, Bangor, Llanfaes, Conway, Rhuddlan, Hull, Flint, Denbigh, Ruthin, Glyndyfrdwy, Chester, Holt, Oswestry, Sycharth, Shrewsbury (Sept—Oct), Welshpool

(b) 1401: Conway, Caernarvon, Ruthin, Welshpool, Cader Idris, Hyddgen, Llanbadarn, Cardigan, Strata Florida, Carmarthen, Llandovery, Builth, Radnor (Sept—Oct), Painscastle, Abergavenny

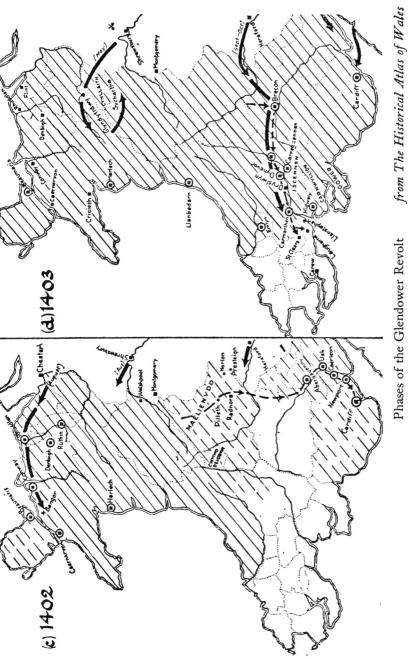

Phases of the Glendower Revolt   *from The Historical Atlas of Wales*

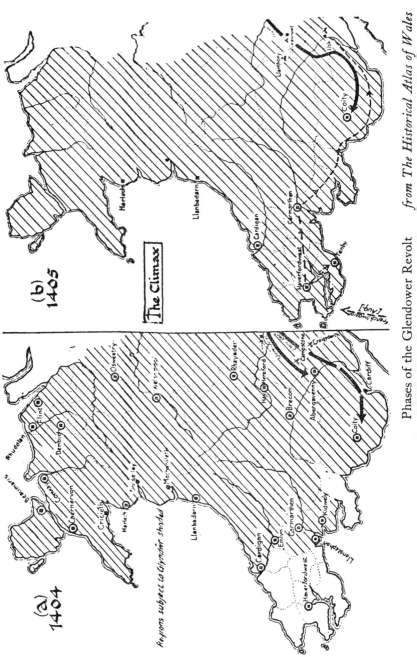

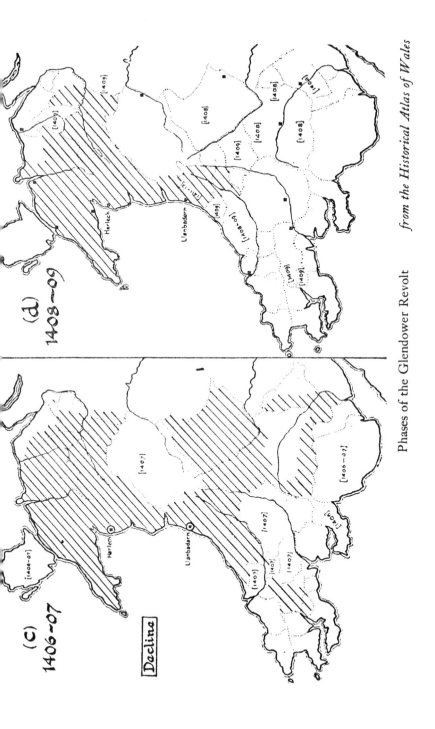

(d) 1408~09

[1409]
[1409]
[1408]
[1408]
[1408]
[1409]
Harlech
[1408]
Llanbadarn
[1408~13]
[1409]
[1408~09]
[1409]
[1409]

(c) 1406~07

Daclina

[1408~07]
Harlech
[1407]
Llanbadarn
[1407]
[1406~07]
[1407]
[1407]
[1407]
[1409]

Phases of the Glendower Revolt   *from the Historical Atlas of Wales* customary to a man of his wealth and status at that time. He had, it seems, the advantage of a wider education than that enjoyed by his neighbours. He had already established a reputation as a soldier and courtier, and he was recognised in Wales and on the Marches as intelligent, popular and generous. And he might have lived out his life in matrimonial contentment, happily supervising his private kingdom, had it not been for one of those ironies of fate with which history is all too replete.

Sometime before Henry IV succeeded in gaining the throne, Glendower had found himself in dispute with a neighbour, Lord Grey de Ruthyn. There had been disagreement concerning a stretch of land, and this had been taken to court. Glendower had no reason to be dissatisfied with the outcome of the case, as the court had ruled that he was the rightful owner of the territory. He was a crown tenant, and Richard II had confirmed the decision of the court. But de Ruthyn was so resentful of the judgment that, taking advantage of the unrest which was provoked by the deposition of Richard II, he had seized and occupied the disputed piece of land.

Glendower appealed to Parliament, but his claim was rejected. If Henry IV was aware of the dispute, he had no time to give it his attention, as he was engaged on the much more urgent business of fighting the Scots. And to prosecute the war he needed the active help of able soldiers. As a crown tenant, Owen Glendower was liable to be called up for military service, and, indeed, a summons was sent requiring him to place himself at Henry's disposal. But the royal command never reached Glendower. De Ruthyn most craftily delayed its delivery in order to prejudice the King against his former comrade.

Concluding that Glendower had refused to serve, Henry IV declared Glendower's lands to be forfeit to the Crown and adding insult to injury, he awarded some of them to the man Glendower now detested, none other than Lord Grey de Ruthyn. This was the series of misunderstandings which resulted in Glendower becoming the focus for an upsurge of Welsh nationalism that was to cause Henry prolonged trouble. It resulted, too, in Glendower being recognised as the ruler of Wales all over the Continent. And it came perilously near to unseating Henry, presenting the English Crown with the most serious uprising since 1066.

Owen Glendower was to prove himself no ordinary foe. Indeed, such were his skills as a leader and a captain, it was claimed that he possessed supernatural powers. In Henry IV, Part I, he was described by Shakespeare as : "The great magician, damn'd Glendower, As well have met the devil alone for an enemy".

Glendower, smarting under a sense of great injustice, reacted to the situation by calling together his friends and tenants and forming them into an armed band. Faced with this act of rebellion, the King ordered De Ruthyn and Talbot of Shrewsbury to capture him. But he not only eluded the force brought against him. On the 16th September, 1400, he attacked Ruthin and some other royal boroughs. News of his successes spread rapidly and produced two opposed reactions The people of Wales recognised in him their champion, while Henry IV issued a proclamation against him. What had started as a private quarrel had swelled to the proportions of an international crisis, with the Welsh people rising against their English monarch. By the summer of 1401 men were pouring in to join Glendower's standard of the red dragon, which had been raised at Plynlimon. And they not only came from all parts of Wales. They came, too, from England. Glendower was being widely proclaimed as the Prince of Wales.

A master of guerilla tactics, he launched lightning attacks on towns occupied by the English, repeatedly defeating the royal forces. When he was so hard pressed he was in danger of capture, he slipped away into the fastnesses of Snowdonia. In West Wales he urged his countrymen to join in "liberating the Welsh race from the bondage of their English enemies". In 1402 he turned his attention to the Welsh Marches, proving so successful that he captured his old enemy, Grey de Ruthyn, as well as the important Marcher Lord, Edmund Mortimer. As generous as always, Glendower allowed de Ruthyn his freedom some time later on payment of a ransom. With Mortimer, he showed insight as well as magnanimity. Mortimer was a younger son in a family whose descent from Edward III caused them to be regarded as a threat to the House of Lancaster.

Glendower saw that an alliance with Edmund Mortimer would provide him with considerable political advantages, and so he arranged that his captive should marry one of his daughters. The making of Mortimer into a son-in-law was a most astute move, for Mortimer was the brother-in-law of Hotspur, the fiery son of Percy Northumberland, who ranked as Henry IV's greatest enemy. With the strength gained from these alliances, and supported by the whole of Wales, Glendower had achieved a position of pre-eminence.

By the end of 1402 he had so firmly established himself that he was able to summon a National Parliament o. Wales, and he called this together at Machynlleth. There he was confirmed as Prince of Wales and there, too, he adopted as his badge the four lions passant of Gwynedd.* His capture of the castle of Harlech and also that of Aberystwyth made him the undisputed master of Wales.

Owen Glendower, who several times proved himself in battle, was much more than a successful guerilla. Primarily, he was a great patriot, and he was a statesman blessed with considerable vision. His education had given him an international outlook, and he realized that he could bring other weapons to bear against Henry besides the instruments of war. Alive to the value of distracting the English, he set about establishing diplomatic relations with England's enemies, France and Scotland. His envoys appeared at foreign courts, negotiations were begun and treaties were made.

His internal policy was naturally directed towards securing the independence of his country and to creating distinctively national institutions. He created a national Parliament and also an independent Church, nominating his own bishops. He also gave attention to the task of providing a Welsh university and to setting up his own law courts. Unhappily, he could not ensure peace for his realm, despite the fact that he remains what many regard as the greatest Welshman in a country whose history is starred with men of immense talent. In his short period of power he revealed himself as a man of vision, possessed of a capacity for government far superior to that shown by any other

---

*See Jacket Cover.

Welshman either before or since.   But the greatest of his
qualities lay in his ability to gain and retain the love of the
people of Wales. His fortunes varied greatly, but throughout all
his vicissitudes he was never betrayed to his enemies nor deserted
by his followers

It was his misfortune that he was required to face the greatest
soldier of his day. This was Harry of Monmouth, who was
Prince of Wales and Henry IV's Lieutenant for the Welsh
territories.   It was a confrontation that caused Glendower
considerable loss and injury. By 1405, helped by the French,
Glendower had been able to go over to the offensive outside
Wales. He advanced into Herefordshire, but his expansion was
shortlived. On the 11th of March one of his armies was routed
at Grosmont, and it was defeated by a much smaller force under
the redoubtable direction of Prince Henry.   This was an
engagement which resulted in Glendower's son and brother
being captured. Worse was to follow. The Welsh leader was
later defeated at Pwll Melyn, in Breconshire, and so resound-
ingly that, for a time, he was a fugitive. There was a further
misfortune when a French fleet, sailing to bring Glendower
reinforcements, was captured by the Cinque Port Squadron.

It is a measure of Owen Glendower's standing and personality
that these reverses, thought highly serious, did nothing to make
him lose the support of his countrymen. The magic of his
name kept alive the national spirit of Wales. He made valuable
use of the protection and strategic advantage provided by the
Welsh hills. Using them as his base, he pursued his guerilla
campaign, keeping the English in a state of tension, as no one
knew where and when he would strike. His operations extended
well into England, whilst he could always retire to the security
of Snowdonia. But, in spite of his skill in warfare, and despite
the faith and determination of his Welsh supporters, he was
losing ground. Prince Henry was such a brilliant commander,
and he used his resources with such skill, that he recaptured the
castles which had fallen to the Welsh and he dealt drastically with
the rebels who fell into his hands.

In spite of these reverses, Glendower was by no means
overthrown. Even in 1409 he was sufficiently strong, although
so much had been wrested from him, to continue the struggle

and even to persuade the Marcher Lords to make truces with him.   In fact, he proved so dogged and determined, that his position in Wales was finally recognized by Henry IV, not formally but tacitly. Glendower was left in peace in Snowdonia, and his influence remained a vital force throughout Wales. And his position was destined to improve, if only for a short time   In 1413 Prince Henry succeeded his father as Henry V. The new King was not looking west towards Wales, but south towards France. His heart was set on conquering that country. Besides, a warrior and a man of courage, he had a great respect for his enemy. Thus he saw it as both politic and honourable to strengthen the peace his father had established with Glendower. And so, before setting out on his French campaign in 1415, Henry sent his former adversary his greetings. He went much further. He offered the Welshman a free pardon, unspoilt by any conditions, and he extended the offer to all Glendower's followers. As proof of his goodwill, he released the son who had been captured at Grosmont.

What reply Glendower made to these royal offers it is impossible to say, as any records that might have been made are no longer in existence. But the great patriot was dying, although the place and manner of his death remain uncertain. According to tradition, he died on the 20th September, 1416, at the home of one of his daughters in the Golden Valley on the Herefordshire border. Whether or not this is true, his place of burial remains a mystery. Many believed as others had believed about King Arthur, that he would come again to lead Wales to independence. It was a conviction that lingered on in the Principality for a long time. Even today, there is no significant part of Wales where his memory is not revered. All over the country there remain items which recall the greatness of Owain Glyndwr. Like other men of genius, he remains an elusive figure in history, but inadequate though the records are, it is evident that this man possessed some of the greatest qualities, and had them in large measure.

His private quarrel with Lord Grey de Ruthyn made him aware of the discontent of his countrymen. Once embarked on the course of rebellion, he had the vision to transform revolt into a national crusade. He realized the need of the Welsh people to express themselves through their own Parliament, their own Church and their own University. He grasped the subtleties and significance of diplomacy, and he turned to his own account the struggle in which the English Crown was engaged to make secure the dynasty of Lancaster. Perhaps it was his supreme achievement to focus the attention of the civilized world on the Principality.

Shakespeare was showing his usual sound judgment when, in *Henry IV*, Part 1, he had Glendower say :

> ' And all the courses of my life do show,
> I am not in the roll of common men '.

X

HARRY OF MONMOUTH
[HENRY V]

1388—1422

' I do believe your Majesty takes no scorn to wear
a leek upon St. David's Day.
I wear it for a memorable honour. For I am Welsh,
you know, a good countryman '.

—SHAKESPEARE, *Henry V.*

THE Prince of Wales who was to ascend the throne as Henry V
had all too short a life. He was, indeed, a man of considerable
and unlike qualities, proving himself in the field of scholarship
and also on the field of battle. Like so many Plantagenet kings,
he showed himself to be a remarkable ruler, far-seeing, progressive and a lover of culture. Compared with many of the
rulers on the Continent, and even with many who were to come
long after him, he was a man of considerable mental and moral
stature.

He was born in Monmouth of exceedingly wealthy and
illustrious parents. His mother was Mary Bohun, and it was
through her that he became heir to vast estates in Wales and also
on the border. His maternal grandfather had been none other
than the redoubtable Humphrey Bohun, a Marcher Lord and
also Prince of Brecknock. The huge Bohun inheritance was
divided between Humphrey's two daughters, Mary and Eleanor
Bohun. The latter married Thomas of Woodstock, uncle of
Henry IV.

The Prince was eleven years old when, in 1399, his father
ascended the throne as Henry IV. Part of his boyhood must have
been spent on the Welsh marches, where he grew to love the
people and admire their martial qualities. He studied at Queen's
College, Oxford, where his education was supervised by his
father's half brother, Henry Beaufort, who distinguished himself
as a great statesman and who served as Bishop of Winchester.

There had been no little controversy as to the legitimacy of the Beauforts, and Richard II had, apparently, settled the matter once and for all when he had Parliament adopt an Act which declared that they were, in fact, legitimate. But the Beauforts were gifted with considerable intelligence, and they continually added to their wealth, influence and power. They did this to such an extent that Henry IV became alarmed and inserted a clause in Richard's Act which debarred them from succession. That the Beauforts had strong claim to the throne seems to be confirmed by Henry Tudor who asserted that he was entitled of his Beaufort blood.

The accession, like the whole reign of Henry IV, was marred by uprisings. Not surprisingly, the Welsh played their part in these troubles. In 1400, when he was not yet twelve years of age, the Prince accompanied his father in the war in Wales. He was with the king in the border fight against Glendower and also when his father dealt with Hotsput's uprising in Shrewsbury.

He was still only in his teens when he revealed that military ability which was to prove such a pronounced quality in his character. He so distinguished himself that he was given independent command in Wales, and he justified his preferment by containing the Glendower rebellion and recapturing the castles which had been lost in the uprising. Although Glendower had shown himself to be an enemy, the Prince preserved for him an immense affection and respect, and he was greatly affected when the rebel died.

His grasp of military matters caused him to be one of the first to appreciate the decisive value of the longbow in the hands of his Welsh countrymen. By 1407, when he was still short of his twentieth birthday, he had virtually completed the task of pacifying Wales. The years that followed remain something of a puzzle to the historian. It was a period in which the Prince gained a reputation for living in a wild and wanton manner. This may have been the case, although what is known of his character does not support the claim. What is more, no contemporary authority of his has offered any evidence, nor even made the accusation, that he lived in a dissolute manner. He may have sown some wild oats, but no more than his father did before him and, so it would appear, not as many as princes of his day were usually allowed to sow without exciting adverse comment.

Throughout the troubled reign of Henry IV, he played his part adequately on the royal Council, and he also discharged the duties of Warden of the Cinque Ports and Constable of Dover. In foreign policy he always favoured an alliance with Burgundy against France.

The relationship between himself and his father was not always as cordial as it might have been, although it is difficult at this late stage to apportion blame for the disagreements that sometimes divided them. There was, apparently, a certain coolness between the two which had its dangers when there were factions struggling over the right to the throne. Enemies of the King, and perhaps secretly of the Prince as well, tried to make the most of this estrangement by suggesting that the Prince should make an attempt to seize the throne. In 1410, in fact, an attempt was made to compel Henry IV to abdicate in his son's favour. Happily, this came to nothing and the pair were reconciled.

By the time he came to the throne—in 1413—he had gained a reputation for being a brave soldier and a brilliant general. But his prowess in the field and his understanding of the subtleties of warfare, had not prevented him from developing an appreciation of music and the arts. A sincere and devoted son of the Church, he carried his passion for orthodoxy to extremes, treating the Lollards and other heretics with a needless severity. But no one could doubt his love and understanding of architecture, furniture and painting, and he proved himself a generous patron of the growing schools of music.

As a soldier he showed himself to be as ruthless in achieving his aim as he was courageous in fighting for it. His tight lips indicate that he was not one with whom it was wise to take liberties, nor even to presume. His religious zeal led him to act cruelly, but, that apart, he was essentially a just ruler.

His father's reign had been plagued by internal struggles, and Henry V understood well the costly nature of fratricidal warfare. He also knew that there was nothing like a common enemy for uniting a people and for diverting mutual distrust and hatred dividing a people into channels where such sentiments were safe and might even be beneficial to the nation. He decided that war with France might serve "to busy giddy minds with foreign quarrels". Thus he was able to satisfy an ingrained hatred and meet national needs by making war on the French. In this adventure he had the support of the Church, but for far from laudatory reasons. The English prelates feared that the young King might enquire too closely into the extent and sources of its worldly possessions. The lords and people of England favoured the royal purpose for equally unworthy motives. They saw in such a war the promise of French loot and much treasure for themselves, and so funds for the venture poured into the royal treasury.

In the year after coming to the throne, Henry V informed the French that he required them to hand over to him the possessions which had been ceded to Edward III at Bretingy in 1360. He also demanded that he should receive the Norman and Angevin lands which, so he said, rightly belonged to England. If these concessions were made, he said, he would then marry Katherine the Fair, and daughter of the feeble minded French monarch, Charles VI.

The French not only rejected these demands, as Henry had known they would, but they did so with an insult. This is one of the many historical events of the period immortalized by Shakespeare, which he tells in the story of the tennis balls sent to the young King. At that time the ball was regarded as a symbol of folly. In their rejection of Henry's proposal the French alluded to the mocking despatch of a ball by Darius, King of the Persians, to the Greek King, and Henry, who had a sound knowledge of the classics, was far from amused by this reference. His reply was typical of the man and proved to be prophetic. "If God so wills and my life lasts", he informed his French maje ty, "I will within a few months play such a game of ball in the Frenchman's streets that this shall lose their jest and gain but grief for their game".

Having given this warning, he set about making ready to carry it out. He planned his expedition with the meticulous care of a great commander. Before setting out on his expedition, he found time to send generous greetings to his old enemy,

Glendower, and to crush a rebellion fomented by his cousin, Richard, Earl of Cambridge, who supported Mortimer in a bid for the throne.

In August, 1415, the English armada set sail from South-ampton. Included in the force were companies of Welsh archers and men at arms, amongst them the Brecknock Archers and detachments from Ystradgynlais. A well known member of the expedition was Dafydd Gam of Newton, Brecon, who had been forced to leave his native town after killing a man in the High Street.

The army landed at Harfleur without encountering oppos-ition, and the great guns, which had been christened ' London ', ' Messenger ' and ' King's Daughter ', battered down the walls of the town. Henry, always seeking the welfare of his subjects, made an attempt to settle the issue without further loss of life by challenging the Dauphin to meet him in single combat. But sickness was reducing the strength of Henry's army, and he decided that delay was likely to prove dangerous. He therefore ordered his army to march to Calais. This move was one which carried his forces right across the front of a French army that was vastly superior in numbers to his own. This army placed itself across Henry's path, and it was obvious that he must fight or suffer defeat and destruction.

On Oct. 25th, 1415—St. Crispin's Day—the French, under D'Albert, joined battle with the English forces. It proved a disastrous and humiliating day for France. For England it wrote into her history the magic name of ' Agincourt ', one of the nation's most memorable victories. The success of the invading forces must be credited—as in the case of Crecy—to the Welsh archers and men at arms. The longbow proved its deadly and decisive nature. But the battle proved to be the last for Dafydd Gam. It is said that he saved the King's life during the engagement, but there is no evidence which either confirms or refutes the claim. But what does appear to be beyond question was Henry's conduct on learning that Gam was dying. The unwelcome news was broken to him in the moment of his victory, and he immediately deserted his nobles, hastened to Gam's side and knighted him. It might well be that it was because of his affection and admiration for Gam

that Henry V, Prince of Brecknock, always showed great
regard for the town of Brecon.

Having set the seal on his qualities as a leader in the field,
Henry returned in triumph to England. But, two years later,
he was once more on the continent, his intention this time being
to conquer Normandy. He pursued a series of engagements
with such tactical brilliance and with an unremitting resolution
that saved him from the danger and disappointment of suffering
a single defeat. His position became so commanding that, in
1420, there was drawn up the Treaty of Troyes. In this he
was declared to be heir of the French King, Charles VI, the
claims of the Dauphin being set aside. The treaty also declared
him to be Regent of the French and Lord of Normandy. It was
then that he honoured his promise and married Katherine of
France. The treaty left no doubt that Henry was a man and a
monarch with whom kings and princes had to reckon.

The treaty, unhappily, did not put an end to hostilities.
Fighting continued intermittently. Thus it was that, in
September, 1422, Henry V died at Bois de Vincennes while on
his way to help his ally, the Duke of Burgundy. Only thirty-
four years of age, he left an infant son, the ill-fated Henry VI.
Katherine of France, who had been married to Henry little
more than two years, later married Owen Tudor and thus
became the grandmother of Henry VII.

Henry V is justly remembered as one of history's great
Captains. His military reputation has tended to obscure his
other achievements and to overshadow his success in other
fields. He was an exceedingly able diplomat, and it was much to
his credit that he brought about the alliance with Burgundy and
Flanders, an agreement which proved of immense benefit to the
English wool trade. He fostered culture and strove to further
education. As a ruler he was firm but just, and he put an end to
uprisings which had cast such a shadow over his father's reign.
Judged by the standards of his day, he was a Christian hero in
that romantic tradition established by King Arthur. He was the
last of the paladins.

In *Henry* VI, Part 1, Shakespeare provided a fitting and
evocative epitaph when he wrote : "Henry the Fifth, too famous
to live long".

XI

THE BUCKINGHAM REBELLION

' Oh let me think on Hastings and be gone
To Brecknock, while my fearful head is on ! '
—SHAKESPEARE, *Richard III.*

HENRY, Duke of Buckingham, lingers in history as a pathetic, illfated figure. His greatest weaknesses were his credulity and excessive ambition. The rebellion to which he gave his name appears now as little more than a foolish gesture, destined to failure even before it was made. It has, however, a larger significance, having some bearing on the coming to power in England of that remarkable royal line—the Tudors.

The rebellion, if it did nothing else, served its purpose as a rehearsal for that invasion of 1485 which was as important as that of the Normans in 1066. For this was the invasion which brought the Tudors to the throne and marked the end of the Middle Ages. It also disclosed that a man who has attained a high and immensely responsible position, can be duped into a course of action that is self destructive.

The shape the Buckingham Rebellion took suggests that its true architect never intended it to succeed. Its whole course indicates that the underlying motive was that of eliminating a rival claimant to the throne that the way might be cleared for Henry Tudor to make his bid for the crown. There is also evidence which points to the conclusion that it was also designed to attract wavering Lancastrians and others who were hostile to the English King—Richard III—to the cause of Henry Tudor, Earl of Richmond. And this was certainly one of the results of the rebellion.

In a sense the Buckingham Rebellion is misnamed. He headed the revolt it is true, but it is equally true that the plot against the throne was not of his conceiving. It was born in the subtle, devious and ruthless mind of John Morton, the Bishop of Ely. Today, the landmarks, Ely Tower and Buckingham Gate, are reminders that it was in Brecknock that the plot was conceived and the plans made for its carrying out.

From earliest times the town of Brecknock had been a place of considerable importance. Commanding the highway from the west the castle, enclosed along with the Priory of St. John, guarded the crossing over the River Usk. Beyond lay the Dominican Friary of St. Nicholas, soon to become after the Reformation the College of Christ of Brecknock, as well as the bridgend hamlet of Llanfaes. But Brecknock had more than a strategic significance. It was the seat of government of the King's Justice and Chamberlain of New and South Wales. This was an office held by Buckingham, who also enjoyed the title of Prince of Brecknock. But his influence and power far transcended these positions. In all the land there was only one man who was more powerful than Buckingham, and that was the King himself. He had achieved this eminence as a reward for the help he had given Richard of Gloucester in his bid for the crown. Without Buckingham's assistance, Richard III would never have gained the heights of monarchy.

Edward IV had died unexpectedly, leaving more than one claimant to the throne, amongst them his younger brother, Richard. This had resulted in a disturbed and difficult situation. The direct descendant of Edward IV was, of course, his son, Edward V, who came to the throne as a minor. Such a position at such a time provided fertile ground for intrigue. The boy-King was too young to exercise the royal power, and the Woodvilles, the relatives of Edward's widow, made strenuous efforts to gain control of the country. Buckingham, however, had remained loyal to Richard, and he had continued to do so when the children of the dead king were declared illegitimate. For his faithfulness Richard had rewarded him lavishly with high offices and the rich estates of Bohun, which he had long claimed as his by inheritance.

Richard III rightly saw in John Morton his most dangerous enemy. A born schemer, Morton had been at the heart of the Hastings Plot against the throne, an act of treason which, normally, would have been punished by death. But Morton was the Bishop of Ely, and his sacred office had caused Richard to decide against sending him to the block. But the Bishop was regarded as too much of a threat to receive a pardon, and he had been placed in Buckingham's custody. The clemency shown him by the King won no gratitude from Morton. He continued to be what he had always been, probably the most able man in the country, subtle of mind and persuasive of tongue, but highly ambitious and a master of intrigue. He had held high office under Edward IV, but in spite of this he had not given the King his undivided loyalty. He had kept in touch with Henry Tudor and with the Lancastrians, with whom his hopes and sympathies resided. So wily and persuasive was Morton that he virtually reversed the roles of warder and prisoner. He exercised such influence on Buckingham that it was the Duke who was receiving suggestions and the Bishop who was leading him to a course that was bound to prove disastrous for the Prince of Brecknock, but by no means so for his mentor.

There can be no doubt that, without the sly incitement of John Morton, Buckingham would never have rebelled. But he was vain and ambitious, a ready prey for Morton's sinister promptings. His claim to the throne was as good as Henry Tudor's, and was perhaps even better, for he traced his descent from Edward III, not only through the illegitimate line of John of Gaunt by way of the Beauforts, but also directly from Thomas of Woodstock. His mother, Margaret Beaufort the younger, had been doubly related as daughter and sister to the Dukes of Somerset—the famous and fiery Beauforts—and Buckingham was thus their legitimate male heir.

There can be no doubt that Morton fed Buckingham's royal ambitions by reminding him of these facts. He must also have pointed out to the Duke that the Act which debarred the Beauforts from assuming the crown did not constitute law and could be set aside if the throne was gained by conquest. These promptings should have been seen to come strangely from a Bishop who favoured Henry Tudor and the Lancastrian cause, but it seems that Buckingham was either unaware of Morton's real motives or was disarmed of all suspicion by the blandishments of his ward.

Even so, the insurrection appears pointless as far as Buckingham was concerned. He had thrown in his lot irretrievably with Richard and the Yorkist cause and had alienated himself from the Woodvilles. By raising the standard of rebellion, he could not count on the support of either faction, and certainly he could expect no help from the Lancastrians. Their cause had become identified with the person of Henry Tudor who, across the Channel, was awaiting a favourable moment to make his own bid for the crown.

The question arises as to why Buckingham was persuaded to embark upon such a forlorn mission. It was an act of folly that was to prove fatal, and it calls to mind the oft-quoted maxim, ' Whom the gods intend to destroy first they make mad '. But Buckingham was blinded by more than the blandishments of John Morton. Ambition, too, served to hide the truth from him. He had tasted power, which is rightly evaluated as the headiest of all wines, and he had also seen with what ease Richard had possessed himself of the throne. He reasoned that, unlike Henry Tudor who was absent on the continent, he, himself, was on the spot. This being the case he would have the better chance of taking advantage of the unrest that would plague the country once Richard had been removed from the throne. It never occurred to him that he was being used by Morton. He did not see that the bishop was even inciting him to a course that would actually further the interests of his rival, Henry Tudor. Indeed, he was so naïve as to believe that Tudor would help to place him on the throne. In this, no doubt, he was misled by Morton, who assured him that Tudor would help him in his purpose by threatening Richard with invasion from the continent. Buckingham certainly did not rebel in order to see his cousin assume the crown. Nor did he live to witness this event. But he helped to ensure that this was precisely what was to come about. His insurrection weakened Richard's position, depriving him, in the person of Buckingham himself, of one who should have been a powerful ally.

In Brecknock Castle the Duke and Bishop plotted against the throne. Buckingham was more a man of action than of words, and he was content to leave the details of the proposed coup to Morton. They were soon in touch with the King's enemies, amongst them, of course, the Woodvilles. Morton now produced a man bearing the name of Reginald Bray, who acted as an intermediary between the Bishop and Henry Tudor's mother, Margaret Beaufort the elder, now the wife of Lord Stanley. It was she who also kept Morton in touch with the Queen Dowager Elizabeth. It was decided that Tudor should sail with a fleet and make a landing on the south coast. Risings, so Buckingham was assured, were to take place in Kent, Surrey and Berkshire under the Woodvilles, while the Duke himself was to march on to London with forces from Wales and unite with the forces of the Courtenays who would approach him from the west.

Plans were hurriedly completed, and October 18th was fixed as the date on which the rebellion was to break out. This, at least, was the arrangement agreed between Buckingham and Morton. But there is reason to believe that the Bishop had other aims. For, in the early days of the month, there were premature risings in several parts of southern England. These occurred before Buckingham had time to complete the mustering of his men, and it is right to wonder if Morton did not deliberately engineer this state of affairs in order to ensure Buckingham's defeat. In any case, the situation proved disastrous for the Duke. News of the revolt was quick to reach the King, and he reacted promptly and with considerable wisdom. He not only levied forces to meet the threat and proclaimed Buckingham a traitor, but he was politic in promising to pardon those rebels who withdrew their support from the Duke at once.

It seemed from the first moment that everyone and everything conspired to bring about Buckingham's undoing. In Wales, Sir Thomas Vaughan and Humphrey Stafford declared for the King, and promptly moved their forces to cut across the route Buckingham was taking to enter England. The King's men smashed the bridges spanning the Severn, thus hindering Buckingham's progress. But it was the weather that delivered the most shattering blow. While still waiting at Brecknock for the men and arms he had been promised, Buckingham became the victim of one of the worst downpours anyone could remember. Torrential rains descended, driven by gale force winds, lashing the whole length of the coast. The floods which resulted became known as the Great Waters, causing the Usk and Severn to rise rapidly, and turning roads and tracks into almost impassable rivers of mud. This delayed the muster from Wales, and it was evident that the rebellion was already a lost cause. But Buckingham was too proud to admit that defeat was even a possibility and he gave no thought to abandoning his purpose. Instead, he dragged his inadequate, soaked and starving army across the sodden lands, trying to find a point at which he could cross the Severn and join up with Courtenay's forces. But the King's supporters had destroyed all the bridges and the swollen waters proved impassable. And in Buckingham's rear, moving up from South Wales, were approaching the forces of Thomas Vaughan.

The Duke's position was also being weakened by deserters. Already the wily Morton, his plan bearing maximum fruit, had slipped away to his diocese in Ely, from where he crossed the Channel to the safety of Flanders. The King's proclamation of clemency was also having its effect. Buckingham saw his numbers dwindling and, at last, he was driven to acknowledge that his rebellion was a failure. He left his son and heir at Weobley with Sir Robert Delebeare, who dressed him as a girl and managed to protect him from Richard's vengeance. Almost alone, Buckingham crept back stealthily to Brecknock Castle, but on reaching it he found that it was in the hands of Thomas Vaughan. Wearing a disguise that for a time proved effective, he wandered from house to house, seeking shelter. And, in Shropshire, he fell victim to a final act of treachery. He was recognised by Ralph Banaster, who might have been expected to afford him help as he was one of the Duke's old retainers. But Banaster, most probably with his eye on possible reward, handed him over to the Sheriff, thus encompassing his doom.

While this was happening, Richard had easily crushed the insurrection in England. As for Henry Tudor's fleet, it had been scattered by the winds. Tudor himself succeeded in reaching the English coast, but he deemed it prudent to sail away without so much as setting foot on land. Most of the principal rebels fled the country and, as Morton had foreseen, added themselves to the forces of Henry Tudor. As was to be expected, the full force of the King's anger was reserved for Buckingham, who had dared to lay rival claim to the throne. The Duke was taken to Salisbury where he was tried and condemned to the block. He was executed the next day, the 2nd of November, 1483. Few men can have risen so high and fallen to their execution so quickly. Less than three months before he paid the price for treason he had held Richard's train at his coronation.

As for Morton, as he had probably intended from the beginning, he joined Henry Tudor, from whom he eventually received his reward for his services when the latter came to the English throne as Henry VII. Morton was made Archbishop of Canterbury in 1486 and he became Chancellor in 1487. But these high offices do not seem to have endeared him to the people. It was he who produced the policy for levying taxes which became unpopularly known as ' Morton's Fork '. Under this, when a subject lived lavishly, Morton claimed that he could afford to pay large tribute to the King as he was obviously wealthy. But the man who lived frugally found himself in no better case. For Morton told him that, as he spent little he must have large reserves, and so he was caught on the other prong of the ' fork '. Morton, in fact, excites little admiration as a statesman, unless cunning and the will to use men to the point of destruction can be counted as virtues. And, as a cleric, the kindest thing that can be said of him is that he made a most astute politician.

Brecknock, it is clear, can justly claim to have played its part in the history of England and Wales. The Buckingham Rebellion and the events it provoked helped to prepare the way for the invasion of 1485, the most important in English history for over four hundred years. This was the excursion headed by Henry Tudor, Earl of Richmond. It was he who defeated and killed Richard III at the Battle of Bosworth Field, and then ascended the throne as Henry VII, and who was the father of England's most remarkable monarch, Henry VIII, and grandfather of the most gifted and dynamic Queen, Elizabeth the First.

XII

THE FIRST TUDOR—HENRY VII
1457—1509

' *My liege, it is young Henry, Earl of Richmond.*
Come hither England's hope—if secret power
Suggest but truth to my divining thoughts
This pretty lad will prove our country's bliss '.
                              SHAKESPEARE, *Henry VI*, Part 3.

HENRY TUDOR, who was to occupy the English throne as
Henry VII, owed much of his success to the untiring efforts of
two people. One was his mother, the Lady Margaret, and the
other was his paternal uncle, Jasper Tudor.

When Henry V died in 1422, his widow, Katherine of
France, ceased to be regarded as a person of importance. She
lived an obscure life far removed from the court. Her son, the
infant Henry VI, was placed in the care of Henry Beaufort,
Bishop of Winchester. During Henry's minority the country
was administered by his uncles. The Royal Council paid
Katherine but scant attention, and the Queen mother was left
pretty much to her own devices. With time on her hands, it
seems that she developed romantic inclinations. In her household was a tall, good-looking and talented Welshman named
Owen Tudor. The Tudors were of sound yeomen stock from
Anglesey, and for many generations the family had been so
gifted as to provide officers for the civil service. An ancestor
who bore the name of Ednyfed Fychan served as the powerful
chief minister of Llywelyn the Great. Another worked closely
with Owen Glendower. The father of Owen Tudor had held
the appointment of Escheator of Anglesey, and had been a
member of the household of the Lord Bishop of Bangor. It was
later claimed that the family could trace its descent from the
ancient royal house of Wales and was in the line of the great
Cadwalladr.

In 1436 Queen Katherine died. It was then discovered that
she and Owen Tudor had been lovers, and that she had borne

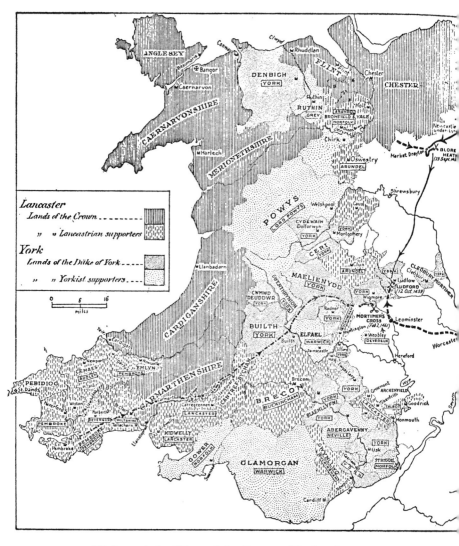

Wales and the Wars of the Roses : York *v* Lancaster
from The Historical Atlas of Wales

sons to her esquire, sons who, of course, were half brothers of the King. It is not surprising that the Council was furious. That the Welshman had shared the Queen's bed was regarded as a slight on the memory of the great Henry V. Owen tried to mitigate the wrath of the Council by claiming that he had been married to Katherine, but when he was required to produce written proof of the wedding he failed to do so, and he was cast into prison. Owen Tudor, however, was very much an optimist and an adventurer. He employed his intelligence to the good purpose of escaping from confinement, and he then produced evidence which satisfied the authorities that he had in fact, been married to Queen Katherine. Eventually Henry VI, a kindly soul, recognised his half-brothers and had them brought up and educated in his court.

We know far too little about the redoubtable and romantic Owen Tudor, who lived an adventurous life. But we do know that he ended his life on the block in Hereford Market after the Lancastrians suffered their disastrous defeat at Mortimers Cross in 1461. He had lived dangerously, and he had managed to survive so many crises that, right until the last moment, he believed that something would happen which would save him his life. When he found himself facing the moment of truth he observed sadly, "That this head should lie on the stock that was wont to lie in Queen Catherine's lap!" His relationship with his wife must have been very tender indeed.

His two sons* had been christened Edmund and Jasper and they prospered in the court of their half brother. And they were awarded titles worthy of men of royal blood. In 1453, Edmund was created Earl of Richmond and Jasper was made Earl of Pembroke. In 1455, Edmund married Margaret Beaufort, the thirteen year old heiress of John Beaufort, 1st Duke of Somerset. There was a son by the marriage, but Edmund did not live to see his birth. The boy was Henry Tudor, and he and his mother were taken into the care of Jasper Tudor.

Napoleon is credited with saying that luck was one of the

---

*There was a third son Owen—a monk.

most important qualities in a man. There can be no doubt that Henry Tudor had a generous amount of this quality. He was certainly lucky in his mother, and he was equally lucky in having such an uncle as Jasper Tudor. Without these two supporting and furthering his aims, he would never have gained the throne. He was lucky, too, in other things, and not least in the Battle of Bosworth Field.

Henry's mother, the Lady Margaret, as she is generally known—and the elder of the two Margaret Beaufort—was one of the most gifted women of her day. She had been well educated and she had that high degree of intelligence, which was such a marked characteristic of the Beauforts. The Beauforts were the family of John of Gaunt by Catherine Swynford. The Beauforts had been declared legitimate by an Act of Richard II. but they had been debarred from the succession by Henry IV. The Lady Margaret was only a year old when her father died. On his death the title of Duke of Somerset passed to her uncle, Edmund Beaufort. She was the first cousin to the other Margaret Beaufort, known as the younger, who was daughter of Edmund, the Second Duke of Somerset. Margaret the younger was mother of Henry, Duke of Buckingham, who claimed to have a stronger title to the crown—through his uncle (Somerset)—than his second cousin, Henry Tudor.

The Lady Margaret married three times. Her first marriage to Edmund Tudor was romantic in origin, and lasted but a short time. She was only seventeen when she married a second time, and again it was affection that prompted the union. Her second husband was Henry Stafford, the brother-in-law of her cousin, Margaret Beaufort, the younger. Her third marriage had a different inspiration. In 1482 she became the wife of Thomas, Lord Stanley, a member of Edward IV's Royal Council. It was Lord Stanley's timely intervention at Bosworth which gave the victory to her son, Henry. It seems fair to conclude that political considerations prompted Margaret to marry Lord Stanley. Apart from the son born to her first husband, she had no other children. And she devoted her whole life to furthering the fortunes of Henry, displaying a singleness of purpose that was of the kind to command success. She was a chief architect in provoking the Buckingham Rebellion, and in the planning of the campaign of Bosworth her part was that of Athene.*

When she had achieved her ambitions, and Henry VII occupied the throne, he did not forget her. He recognised the part she had played in achieving the crown by having her raised to the position of the first lady of the land. The Lady Margaret, in fact, was accorded far more respect than was her daughter-in-law, the Queen Elizabeth of York. But she was concerned with other things besides position and power. She was deeply interested in education and, during the reign of Henry VII, she spent no little time founding colleges both at Oxford and Cambridge. Perhaps even more important in the world of education was the contribution she made by acting as one of the early patrons of Caxton. Her memorial at Westminster, the lovely bronze and marble by Pietro Torrigiano, bears testimony to her grandson's gratitude and devotion to one who was a woman of parts and of commendable ideals. She died in 1509, highly and widely esteemed.

The Wars of the Roses present that unhappy spectacle of a house divided against itself. It is hardly surprising, therefore, that the period was not noted for expressions of family loyalty. Indeed, a shadow that lingers over the constantly changing scene is the enmity and treachery relatives displayed for one another. A most welcome change from this all too common pattern is found in Jasper Tudor. He stands out as an example of unswerving and unselfish devotion to the fortunes of a relative ; in his case to one who was no more than his brother's son.

When his sister-in-law married Henry Stafford, Henry Tudor was placed in the care of his Uncle Jasper. He was surrounded by Welsh nursemaids, and it is fair to assume that he heard tales of the ancient Welsh Princes. From the beginning of the Wars, Jasper Tudor played a prominent part in organising support for the Lancastrian cause in Wales. He remains in history as an elusive figure, but there can be no doubt that he left a great impression on his generation. He was extremely

*Athene, identified by the Romans with Minerva, was the embodiment of wisdom.

popular and enjoyed the all-important support of the bards, who wrote of him :

> ' Jasper will breed for us a dragon—
> Of the fortunate blood of Brutus is he—
> A bull of Anglesey to achieve
> He is the hope of our race '.

In the difficult field of public relations Jasper did a magnificent job for his nephew.

In 1461 he raised an army in Wales. It was his intention to join up with the royal forces in the north, which, under Somerset, were marching on London. But he was prevented from achieving his purpose. At Mortimers Cross, on the Herefordshire border, he came face to face with young Edward of York, who was to distinguish himself as a brilliant commander. On 10th February, 1461, Jasper Tudor suffered a crushing defeat at the hands of Edward, who was, of course, the future Edward IV, the first English King to have the blood of Llywelyn the Great in his veins. Edward, a clever strategist and courageous warrior, understood the need to instil into his men the will to fight. To boost the morale of his troops he claimed to have seen three suns over the battlefield. After his victory in the battle he incorporated the blazing sun into his badge of the white rose of York. Jasper, the victim of defeat, was lucky to escape from the field and go into hiding. He spent some months, along with his nephew, Henry, avoiding his enemies by concealing himself in the Welsh mountains.

This began for Jasper a period of misfortune. In September, 1461, Pembroke Castle fell and, by attainder, he was deprived of his earldom. The title was awarded to William Herbert, a friend of Edward IV. Jasper again fled, this time abroad. During the next few years he acted as a rallying point for those Welshmen who were opposed to the Yorkists. He was with Warwick the Kingmaker in 1470, when England was successfully invaded and, for a short time, Henry VI was restored to the throne.

In 1471 he was busy rallying the Welsh to the cause of Lancaster. But he was destined to suffer disappointment once more. For some reason which history fails to explain, he failed to reach Tewkesbury in time to save the Lancastrians from a crushing defeat. Learning of the disaster, he joined his nephew at Chepstow and, after a series of adventures in which their lives were in danger, they succeeded in reaching the coast and boarding a ship. But his misfortunes were not yet over. It was Jasper Tudor's intention to sail to France, but either because of treachery or due to poor seamanship, they were put ashore at Brest. This meant that they were in Brittany, which was under the rule of Duke Francis, and he was well aware of the changed position in which the young Henry Tudor now found himself. Francis accepted them ostensibly as guests, but, in reality, they were his prisoners.

Soon after Tewkesbury, King Henry VI was murdered, and his death had far-reaching consequences. The direct line of Lancaster was destroyed, and so, too, was the direct male line of the House of Beaufort. Henry's death left only two plausible Lancastrian claimants. Both were Henrys and both made their claim because of their links with the House of Beaufort. One was, of course, Henry Tudor, and the other was his second cousin, Henry Stafford, Duke of Buckingham. It seemed unlikely that Buckingham would make a bid for the throne. He was under the eye of the King, and he had also been married to the Queen's sister, Catherine Woodville.*

During his years in exile Jasper supervised the education and guided the way of life of his nephew. At the same time he kept alive Henry's ambitions to the throne, insisting that he was the most plausible Lancastrian claimant. He was also busy preparing the ground for the successful bid for the crown, which was made in 1485. There can be no doubt that, throughout these years, he was in touch with the Lady Margaret and it is likely that he preserved contact with John Morton, the Bishop of Ely.

Edward IV was well aware that Henry Tudor presented a threat to the throne, and it was only natural that he should seek to neutralise him. To this end, he made repeated efforts and made him several most attractive offers in the hope of enticing him back to England. But, on each occasion, Jsaper Tudor persuaded his nephew that he would be unwise to accept. And while safeguarding Henry, Jasper Tudor was also busy clearing

*Later she became Jasper Tudor's wife.

the way for the bid for the throne. The part he played in the Buckingham Rebellion and in the invasion of 1485 are dealt with elsewhere in this volume. But he had a decisive hand in both these events.

When Richard III succeeded to the throne in 1483, he was as much aware of the threat to his crown emanating from Henry Tudor as Edward IV had been. In fact, in 1484, he made a bid to capture Henry or, at least, to restore him to full custody in Britanny. It was an attempt that came near indeed to succeeding. It was foiled by Jasper Tudor, who had been warned of the plot by the ever reliable John Morton. Acting on the information received from Morton, Jasper Tudor was able to warn Henry just in time for him to shake off his pursuers and cross the border into France.

The following year he landed at Milford Haven with his nephew and was at his side at the Battle of Bosworth Field. He was rewarded for his fidelity and his considerable services in a befitting manner. He was restored to the earldom of Pembroke, created Duke of Bedford, and appointed Lord of Glamorgan and Justiciar of South Wales. His wife, Catherine Woodville, was the aunt of Elizabeth of York, Henry VII's Queen.

Jasper Tudor is one of the most attractive characters in Welsh history. Without his loyalty to the Tudors and his planning on Henry's behalf, it is almost certain that Henry Tudor would never have attained the English throne, but it seems that his vital services have gone almost unnoticed. He had all the high qualities which go to the making of a gentleman of Wales. He died in 1495, a much honoured and much loved elder Statesman.

Henry Tudor was born at Pembroke Castle in 1457. The Wars of the Roses had started on their erratic and uncertain course two years before, and he was identified both from his father and mother with the cause of Lancaster. From his earliest years he was caught up in the upheavals of the era, and his fortunes were firmly linked with those of his devoted uncle, Jasper. It was Jasper who cared for him as an infant, but when Pembroke Castle fell in 1461, Henry was taken into the household of William Herbert, to whom the Earldom of Pembroke had been transferred. It was the intention of the Herberts to marry him to their daughter, and had this happened his chances of gaining the throne would have been greatly diminished. But Herbert was killed by Warwick in 1469, and the following year Jasper Tudor returned and once more took Henry into his care. Jasper took the boy to Westminster to see Henry VI and to urge that the title of Earl of Richmond, which had been forfeited in the attainder of 1461, should be restored to him. But this was something Warwick was unable to do, as it had been granted to his son-in-law, Clarence, at that time his ally.

Between 1471 and 1483 Henry Tudor became a pawn in the devious game of European diplomacy. It was very much in the interests of Edward IV to have Henry returned to England, but he could not persuade Duke Francis of Brittany to hand Henry over. All that Edward could obtain from Francis was the unsatisfactory promise that Henry would not be allowed to leave Brittany. Edward IV was not afraid of Henry, but he would have been happier to have him where he could keep an eye on him. In his efforts to persuade Henry to take up residence again in England, Edward promised him safe conduct and offered him brilliant marriages and enviable titles. Henry's position was far from satisfactory. During all his years in exile he had to be wary of treachery, and he had little prospect of an upward turn in his fortunes. He had, however, two advantages over his second cousin, Buckingham. He was unmarried, and was therefore free to make any matrimonial contract which promised to be beneficial to him. And, although he was dependent on the goodwill of Francis, who was his ' host ', he was not under the control of Edward. Also, his mother and uncle Jasper were making subtle use of propaganda to build him up as the hope of the House of Lancaster.

The position of Henry changed dramatically in 1483, when King Edward died suddenly at the early age of forty. The Lady Margaret had just contracted her third marriage, and to none other than Thomas, Lord Stanley. He was a powerful Yorkist magnate in the North West and a member of the Royal Council. Edward IV's early death had left a vacuum at the very centre of power, his two heirs, Edward V and Richard of York, being the minors. In such a situation, intrigue and attempts to seize the throne were almost inevitable, and the Woodville Plot, the Hastings conspiracy to seize the crown, involved Lord Stanley.

However, he was pardoned, and so a doubtful ally of Henry Tudor's was spared. And the path to the throne was further cleared for him by the disclosure of the precontract of marriage between Edward IV and the Lady Eleanor Butler, as such an engagement was regarded as tantamount to marriage itself. Edward's two children were declared illegitimate by Act of Parliament, and the crown passed to Richard III. Henry had little chance of gaining the throne while Edward was alive, but the position was very different the moment that Richard assumed the crown. There were many powerful individuals and bodies who chose to regard Richard as a usurper, and there were many who were willing to see Richard in this guise because they had felt for Edward, the father of the Princes in the Tower, a deep regard and affection.

Henry Tudor's position was strengthened because he was able to attract to his standard not only Lancastrians and Woodvilles—himself being of the House of Lancaster—but he could also gain the support of Yorkists as well. These were men who were not in sympathy with the kind of rule imposed by King Richard. Inevitably, because power and possessions were distributed in the way they were, there were several men in high places who had a vested interest in seeing Richard deposed.

It was My Lord of Buckingham, so lacking in political insight, who had placed Richard III on the throne. And it was he, too, who provoked the uprising which started the chain of events which were to result in Henry Tudor gaining the throne. On Christmas Day, 1483—the year in which the Buckingham Rebellion had failed so disastrously for its leader—Henry Tudor took a public vow in Angers Cathedral, Brittany, that he would marry Elizabeth of York. This was a shrewd move, designed to strengthen his bid for the throne. Aware of this, Richard redoubled his efforts to capture Henry, but in this he failed, Henry managing to flee into France.

Henry Tudor could do little but wait while, in England and Wales, the agents of his mother and his uncle were making ready for his return. Their efforts were causing a trickle of supporters to fill his ranks. On the 22nd August, 1485, the crown which had fallen from the head of Richard III at Bosworth Field was retrieved by Stanley and transferred to the

head of Henry Tudor. The following year, Henry Tudor
somewhat tardily made good his vow by marrying Elizabeth of
York. In *Richard III* Shakespeare said of the contract :

'We will unite the white rose and the red :
Smile Heaven upon this fair conjunction,
That long hath frowned upon their enmity !
What traitor hears me, and says not Amen ? '

From his earliest boyhood, Henry Tudor had learned to live
with suspicion and treachery. He had lived abroad, and for so
long that he was virtually a foreigner. He had, too, gained the
throne by the right of conquest. He was well aware that he had
many enemies, real and potential, and he was determined to
ensure that they did not combine against him to rob him of his
crown. He decided that any sign of weakness might prove fatal
to his position. Although he was not unmindful of his Welsh
associations and of his debt to the people of Wales, he evinced
but scant interest in trying to win the respect or affection of his
English subjects. He pursued a policy designed to keep the
people—nobles and commoners alike—in a compliant frame of
mind. Inevitably perhaps, his position being what it was, there
were disorders and uprisings during his reign. Nevertheless, his
throne was never seriously threatened, and he continued to
pursue, if not in quite the same way, the policies of his Yorkist
predecessors.

His reign, it is generally agreed, was one of considerable
achievements. Through his Chancellor, John Morton—
famous and hated on account of his ' Fork '—he reorganised
the finances so that the crown was enriched and the economy
was strengthened. He so developed the machinery of government that he increased the power of the central authority—the
crown. And he so disposed justice and law that they imposed
on the people an iron despotism. Nevertheless, when he died
at the end of a reign that laster almost a quarter of a century,
he had vastly reduced the power of the barons and Marcher
Lords, who had enjoyed and often abused an excessive authority
far too long. In this way, he had cleared the path for changes
which, though still much in the future, were to prove beneficial
to the people as a whole. He had, too, amassed an enormous
fortune for the crown.

The victory of Bosworth and the accession of a Welshman to
the English throne seemed to give substance to the prophecies of
the Welsh bards that Wales would shake off England's overlordship. The fact that Welshmen were very numerous and
well received at court seemed to lend confirmation to this view.
But it was to prove false. Henry was preoccupied with the
task of maintaining his position against the many Yorkists who
believed that they were more entitled to the throne than he
was. It was a royal prepossession that spilled over into the reign
of Henry VIII and it prevented the emergence of any separate
policy for Wales.

The Welsh gentry merchants and artists found themselves
looking to London as the centre of culture and trade. This
broke that paternalistic pattern which had embraced all classes
and which had been such a feature of society in Wales. The
landowners lost touch with their people. There emerged two
nations in a Wales which was developing in a manner quite
different from that envisaged by Owen Glendower. There is,
indeed, a hint of irony in the fact that the accession of a Welshman to the throne of England was the real cause of the loss of
independence for Wales. Although inspired by the best of
motives, the Acts of Union inspired by Henry VIII put an end
to all hopes of Welsh independence.

XIII

THE PATH TO BOSWORTH

AUGUST 1485

' Sound drums and trumpets boldly and cheerfully.
God and Saint George ! Richmond and victory ! '
—SHAKESPEARE, *Richard III.*

THE Buckingham Rebellion, with its ironic and tragic overtones,
served as a prelude to the events of 1485. Towards the end of
1483, Henry Tudor had made a vow that he would marry
Elizabeth of York. This was a move of high political importance. Such a contract drew to Henry's standard support of a
nature that promised to be decisive. Before the vow was made,
he had little hope of gaining the throne. But the vow meant
that he was in a position to seriously challenge Richard III and
to make a formidable effort to assume the crown.

Henry's solemn promise to marry Elizabeth of York made it
imperative for him to leave Brittany. He had made his first
move in a bid for the throne. Now he made his second. He
escaped to France, not only to take himself beyond Richard's
reach, but also to prepare his campaign against the king. He
set up headquarters at Rouen, and to him came those Lancastrians and Yorkists, as well as members of the Woodville family
who felt they had reason to oppose the English king At first,
their numbers were small, but he gained help of considerable
importance when he was joined by John de Vere, Earl of
Oxford, who had escaped imprisonment by Richard. Oxford
was not only a man of great influence, he was also a capable
and experienced commander.

Meanwhile, Henry Tudor was active on his own behalf.
He was in contact with the French King, seeking to persuade
him to give practical help. In this he was encouraged by the
knowledge that the French monarch was related to him, as
Henry was the grandson of Katherine of Valois. Henry's
mother, too, was working on his behalf. Through her agents

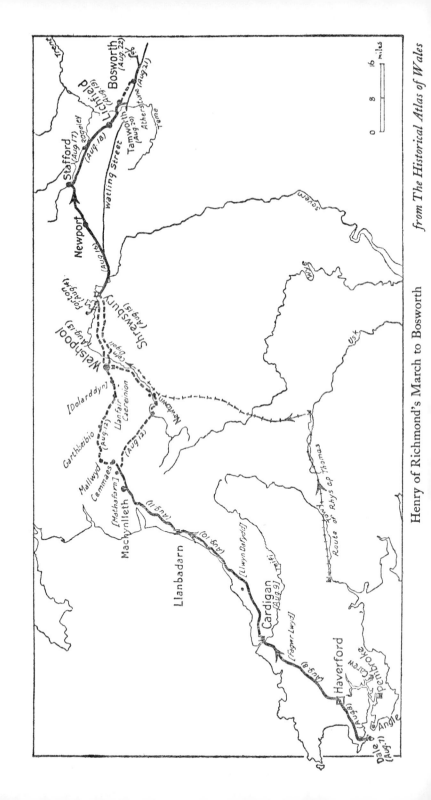

Henry of Richmond's March to Bosworth

from The Historical Atlas of Wales

he was in touch with leading personalities in Wales. Instigated by Jasper Tudor, a propaganda campaign was being conducted amongst the Welsh, the instruments of publicity being the Welsh bards, and it was having considerable success.

It was one of Lady Margaret's agents, a Dr. Lewis, who advised that Henry Tudor would be wise to invade the country, by making his entry at Milford Haven, in Pembrokeshire. It proved to be a fortunate suggestion. Whether it was Dr. Lewis's intention to mislead Richard III's agents, or whether they simply made a mistake, the fact stands that they passed on the wrong information. In 1483, Henry Tudor had attempted to effect a landing at another Milford, on that occasion at the one in Dorset that lay close to Poole And it seems that Richard's agents believed a second attempt was to be made in the same place

There were, however, obvious advantages for Henry Tudor in making his landing in Wales. Not least was the fact that he was a Welshman. Of equal importance was the mood of the people themselves. They longed to shake off the English yoke, and so Henry was justified in assuming that he would be received on Welsh territory with sympathy and, perhaps, with enthusiasm. There were other stretches of the coast which would not afford him a welcome. The ill-conceived and disastrous Buckingham Rebellion had revealed that Richard III was secure North of the River Thames and East of the River Severn. But the Welsh were sympathetic, as they always had been, to the cause of Lancaster. And the indefatigable Reginald Bray, always active on Henry's behalf, was, so reports claimed, meeting with success in raising funds for the Tudor cause.

In the spring of 1485, Queen Anne, wife of Richard III, died. It was rumoured that the King intended to marry his niece, Elizabeth of York. Had this happened, the position of Henry Tudor would have been considerably changed for the worse. But, if this was Richard's intention, nothing came of it, and the reassuring news that there was to be no such alliance prompted Henry to press forward with his preparations for invading the country. He was further encouraged in his intentions by the information passed to him by the Welsh lawyer, John Morgan. He was able to report that Sir John

Savage and Rhys ap Thomas, men of considerable importance in South Wales were eager to give him their support. He received, too, a promise of support from his step-father, Lord Stanley, who said that he would give what help he could to his wife's son. Lord Stanley was a man of power, being the magnate both in Cheshire and the North West. His brother, Sir William Stanley, was Chief Justice of North Wales and was the power in Denbigh and Shropshire.

The Stanleys had served as most accurate pointers to the outcome of events for quite some time. Since 1459, victory in the Wars of the Roses had favoured one side and then the other. But, always, as if gifted with second sight, the Stanleys had managed to identify themselves with the winning side.

In spite of John Morgan's report that Rhys ap Thomas had promised to give Henry Tudor his support, he made a vow to Richard III that Henry Tudor would gain victory only "over my belly". But this, as events were to prove, was a vow made only to mislead the monarch.

The French, scenting success, now promised to give support to Henry, offering him fifteen ships and 2,000 men, as well as money. Whatever the worth of the ships and the money, the men were a most doubtful advantage. They were recruited from the gaols of Normandy, being convicts who were promised their freedom on condition that they took part in Henry's invasion. They were described by a contemporary chronicler, and almost certainly with considerable justice, as "A most evil lot".

By the end of July the preparations for the enterprise were complete. Losing no time, the fleet sailed on the 1st August. In addition to the French contingent there were 500 exiles, and the commanders, in addition to Henry Tudor, were Jasper Tudor and the Earl of Oxford. Richard's fleet was patrolling the Channel, but the French vessels avoided it by taking a westward course. On 7th August an unopposed landing was made at Dale, in the great bay of Milford Haven. At Haverfordwest, six miles to the north east, Jasper Tudor received the reassuring news that Pembroke Town had declared for Henry. But there was other news which was by no means so cheerful. He was told that, although both Rhys ap Thomas and

Sir John Savage had mustered their forces, they had not declared their loyalty. In view of the uncertainty created by this information, Henry decided to move north west to Cardigan, and the garrison there surrendered.

It was at this point that John Morgan, shrewd and far-seeing, suggested that Henry should make Rhys ap Thomas a generous offer. Accordingly, a message was sent to Rhys promising him the Lieutenancy of all Wales in return for his support. It now became clear that the Welshman's vow to Richard had been an empty promise. Whatever his intentions when assuring the King of his support, he now revealed that he could break his word readily and by means of a patent subterfuge. He lay under a bridge over which Henry Tudor rode, and so the invader had, in fact, "passed over my belly". Assured of the support of Rhys, Henry was now free to move more deeply into the country. With South Wales secure, he sent Rhys eastward to raise the standard of the Red Dragon throughout Carmarthen and Brecon.* Henry, himself, marched directly through Wales and, under the banner of the Red Dragon, crossed the River Severn at Shrewsbury. The men, a mixture of French, English and Welsh, marched to the song of ' The Bull of Anglesey ', someone caustically remarked of Henry, "With a train of Welsh myth streaming behind him and proclamations shooting out before".

Messages were sent out by Henry Tudor commanding all who received them. And they were signed prematurely and with no little effrontery, "By the King" ! It is true that men did respond to his summons, but they did not do so in considerable numbers, and there was no popular rising. Also of no little concern to Henry was the fact that the Stanleys—who could choose sides so readily and change course so quickly, had not yet committed themselves. And, because of their power and resources, these two men were in a position to decide the issue.

On 13th of August Henry Tudor reached Shrewsbury. It was there that he was met by Reginald Bray, who handed over the money he had raised in Wales. It was there, too, that he met the two Stanleys. Lord Stanley had 4,000 men stationed to

---

*The standel at Llanddew, Brecon, marks one of the rallying points.

the east of the town, while, to the north east, Sir William
Stanley had 2,500 men awaiting his orders. Between them they
mustered what promised to be a decisive force. In spite of this,
they refused to commit themselves. But they were free—and
persuasive—with their advice. It had been Henry's original
intention to move directly on London. But the Stanleys urged
him to bring Richard to battle before his muster was complete.
And the King was not in London. He had made Nottingham
his headquarters during the invasion season. And so Henry
made a change in his plans. Instead of marching on London, he
made towards Newport.

Richard's agents had kept him informed of the preparations
being made at Harsfleur to invade his kingdom, and his fleet
had been posted to cover the south coast. But Richard had too
few friends in Wales, and he received but scant information from
that quarter. Henry's forces had been in the country a week
and had reached Shrewsbury before Richard learned of their
landing. On hearing where his enemy was, he decided that
Henry would debouch from Wales into Herefordshire, and he
sent out orders instructing his principal captains to rendezvous
at Leicester.

On August 15th Richard received news that must have
caused him some degree of anxiety. Thomas Stanley pleaded
that he could not obey the King's command to bring his muster
to Leicester due to the fact that he was ill. On the same day the
young Stanley, who bore the title of Lord Strange, tried to slip
out of Nottingham. This attempted act of desertion must have
convinced Richard that Thomas Stanley's plea of sickness was
false. He must have realised that the Stanleys were more than
likely to give their support to his enemy. And this was confirmed
when Lord Strange broke down under interrogation and
revealed that not only his uncle, but also Sir John Savage and
Rhys ap Thomas, as well as others, had agreed to join Henry
Tudor.

Richard III must have felt that he faced a dangerous situation.
The Buckingham Rebellion had left a gap in the western
defences which had not been filled, and Henry Tudor had made
the most of this opening in his invasion of the country. News
now arrived that Henry had reached Shrewsbury without

encountering opposition and was moving towards Nottingham. Richard also learnt that Henry was now advancing with the support of Talbot of Shrewsbury, who had added some 500 men to Tudor's forces. Talbot felt that he had two compelling reasons to hate the King. He was married to the daughter of Hastings, an earl who had been executed by Richard III. And he blamed the King for making known the precontract, and so exposing to the world the shame of his relative, Eleanor Butler.

When, on the 17th of August, Henry Tudor reached Lichfield, he was under the surveillance of the King's mounted scouts. He had again changed direction in order to move down Watling Street. Two days later, no less than six different armies were converging on Leicester. There was King Richard's own army, which had left Nottingham. Behind him came the laggard Percy of Northumberland and his men. He had the same hesitant and cautious attitude towards the coming battle which the Stanleys were displaying. A third army was under the Duke of Norfolk, who was loyal to the King, and who was leading his force across England. Approaching from a different direction—the West—and only a few miles apart, were the soldiers of the two Stanleys. Finally, there was the sixth army, that of Henry Tudor. It can hardly be doubted that there had never been a more curious military situation. Of the six forces approaching one another, three were not finally committed to either of the leading protagonists, and it was these forces which had the power to decide the issue.

When it came to displaying courage it seems fair to judge that Richard was superior to his Tudor opponent. All the evidence attests that he moved boldly to join issue with his enemy. Not so Henry Tudor. When his army had proceeded beyond Lichfield, he had remained in the town and for obvious reasons. The shelter of Wales was receding and capture or defeat could mean only one thing—death. His scouts, too, had provided him with discouraging news. Richard, they had reported, seemed well prepared for battle and his forces were superior to those committed to Henry. Apart from Talbot and those who had pledged to fight with Tudor he had received little of the support he had been led to expect before leaving France. Nevertheless, he could count on the assistance of the

Earl of Oxford and Jasper Tudor and he had no choice but to set out to join them. While still on his way, darkness fell and he mistook his course. Which explains why it was not until dawn on August 20th that he managed to rejoin his allies, who, by this time had become anxious as to his whereabouts.

It was on this day that he met the Stanleys. And it seems that he did not receive the assurances that he both desired and expected. The Stanleys made it clear that they wished Henry well. They preferred to see him on the throne rather than Richard. Nevertheless, they were determined—as always—to be on the winning side. In the end, that was the side they were on. But they were to pay dearly for their hesitation. Their tardiness in committing themselves to Henry's cause was neither forgotten nor forgiven. Although Lord Stanley was created Earl of Derby for the sake of Lady Margaret, he was never again allowed to hold office. As for Sir William Stanley, he paid the supreme penalty for what Henry regarded as his failure at a most crucial moment. When opportunity occurred, Henry had him executed.

On 21st of August, Henry Tudor marched down Watling Street. Meanwhile, Richard's forces took up a position near Market Bosworth, with Northumberland still following slowly in his rear. By nightfall the armies were clustered about a rise known as Ambien Hill. When the two armies faced each other at dawn the following day, their approximate strength was such that the balance appeared to be in Richard's favour. In addition to the 6,000 men under his command there were 3,000 more under the Earl of Northumberland. Against them, Henry Tudor had brought the 2,500 men who had landed with him at Milford Haven, plus some 2,000 men who had joined his standard on the march through Wales. There were, too, the 500 men under the Earl of Shrewsbury—some 5,000 in all. But the decisive forces were stationed on the flanks of the opposing armies. Still not committed to either side, there were Lord Stanley's 4,000 men and Sir William Stanley's force of 2,500.

Battle was joined when the force under the Earl of Oxford launched an attack on the Duke of Norfolk. At the same time, Thomas Stanley moved his 4,000 men towards the position held by Northumberland. Oxford's attack was repelled by the Duke of Norfolk, and he was compelled to fall back.

The battle had been in progress for little more than half an hour when it was reported to the King that Henry Tudor, Jasper Tudor and the standard of the Red Dragon, carried by William Brandon, could be seen on the slope behind Oxford's wing. Richard realised that the issue could be settled only if he succeeded in striking down Henry Tudor. To come to grips with Henry, Richard had to ride across the front of the forces commanded by Sir William Stanley. This involved taking a calculated and justifiable risk, but it could only succeed if Henry was brought down in the minimum of time.

Richard decided that the best course was to launch an attack himself at the head of a small body of his own household. The horses were brought up and the fateful order was given, "We ride to seek Henry Tudor !" At the head of a hundred men, Richard charged, and it was a move that came within an ace of succeeding. The Red Dragon was cut down, William Brandon losing his life. It was at this most critical of moments that William Stanley at last decided to take a hand. He drove in from the flank on to Richard's men. Not only was the King killed, but most of his household also lost their lives.

Reginald Bray found the crown—a chaplet of gold worn round Richard's helmet—under a hawthorn bush. And it was one of the Stanleys, probably Thomas, who placed it on the head of Henry Tudor. So ended the Battle of Bosworth Field, one of the most decisive in the history of the country. Richard III was the last King of the House of York, and Henry VII was the first of the Tudor dynasty. August 22nd, 1485 marked the beginning of a new era in the history of England and Wales

XIV

THE ACTS OF UNION

1536 AND 1542

THERE are many ironies in Welsh history, but none to equal what many Welshman regard as the most repugnant of all. It was a Welshman, Henry VIII, who was responsible for Wales losing her independence. It was his enactments which united Wales with England, fastening upon her English rule.

It was the settled policy of the Tudors to crush the over mighty barons. This was as much a progressive necessity as a political necessity. And it meant that it was the power of the Lords Marcher which was to be curtailed, as they provided the hard core of the baronial tradition, and they had, for generations, fomented trouble for the English crown. In Wales the King's writ was held in scant regard, and the Tudors were determined to change this state of affairs. This meant fusing the two nations into one, but at the expense of the Welsh. Wales was to become a part of England, and Welshmen were to be compelled to adopt English ways and customs. They were, in fact, to be turned into Englishmen.

Henry VIII's Act of Union decreed that English was to be the only official language of Wales. To ensure that this was so, no Welshman unable to speak English could hold any government office. The system of land inheritance, which divided up a holding between all the legitimate sons of the father, was replaced by the English system of inheritance which was based on primogeniture. The 'sinister usages and customs' of Wales were to be extirpated. Counties were created that all the country might lend itself to the same type of administration, and provision was made for the counties and county boroughs to be represented at Westminster. As Wales had never developed any sort of a national assembly the question of a separate Parliament did not arise.

Since the Act of Union incorporated Wales into England no national boundary was regarded as necessary. Districts were dealt with in an arbitrary manner. Oswestry, for instance, which was Welsh by tradition and language, was blandly placed in Shropshire ! Under the Tudors, the Welsh gentry and merchants looked to London as the centre of culture, patronage and business, it was decided that Wales had no need of a capital city. It is this lack of a metropolitan city which would have furnished a centre for the national culture and as a focus for her national spirit which has provided the main hindrance for the development of Wales. Geography, too, has proved a stumbling block, and has done throughout the history of the Principality.

Today, however, it seems that Wales is on the way to achieving individuality. In 1955, Cardiff was designated as the country's capital city. In 1964 a Secretary of State for Wales was created, and he was given the status of Cabinet rank. And, at the time of writing, the people seem determined to procure by democratic means a Wales that has dominion status. Perhaps the dreams of Llywelyn the Last of Welsh independence are about to be realised. It may be that the Prince of Wales who is to be presented to the Welsh people in 1969 will prove to be the first of a long line of Princes who is the royal link between two separate nations bound together by ties of mutual help and regard. It is a prospect that has some encouraging possibilities.

XV

WALES AND THE CIVIL WARS

1642—1649
1745

WHEN the Civil War broke out in England in the seventeenth century the territories which favoured the King, on the one hand, and Parliament on the other, could be defined with a reasonable degree of accuracy. The dividing line might have been drawn from Hull to Gloucester and then on to Plymouth. The people to the north and west of the line favoued the King, while those to the south and the east supported Parliament. Such a line would, of course, be of a somewhat arbitrary nature, as more than geographical location separated the conflicting forces. There were social divisions which were likely to transcend the place of birth and domicile. It could be said, for instance, that the aristocracy, squirearchy and peasantry supported the royal cause, while the professional classes, merchants and substantial farmers sympathised with the Roundheads.

Even these distinctions fail to complete the ways in which the protagonists grouped themselves. Religion played an often decisive part. High Churchmen and Catholics tended to approve of royalty, while dissenters were more than likely to give their loyalty to the Puritans. But, as in all human disputes involving large numbers of people, there were those in one camp who might, because of their nationality, economic or social position, or religion, have been expected to be in the other.

The Welsh, as might be expected, were almost unanimously royalist. The Tudors had supplied the English throne with monarchs for over a hundred and fifty years, or with Kings who had Welsh blood in their veins. This fact proved of little worth to the Principality. The Tudors may have shown a partiality for Welshmen, but not for Wales as a whole, and the Stuarts certainly showed no particular friendship for the country.

Although royalty may have failed to grant the Welsh any

special advantages, or even any benefits of any kind, Parliament had aroused the disdain and hostility of almost all Welshmen. The fact that it was remote and foreign excited suspicion. But it was blamed for the Act of Union which had forbidden the use of the Welsh language in all official documents and dealings. It was seen as responsible—as, indeed, it was—for the laws which forbade attendance at Mass, and it had won no little unpopularity because of the way it had altered the system of inheritance.

The impact of the Reformation on Wales had been negligible. The religion centred in Rome still struck a deep response in Welsh hearts. Puritanism, with its lack of poetry and symbolism, struck no chord in the hearts of a people who cherished romance, song and the stimulating products of the imagination. There were still no printing presses in Wales, and this left the field clear to the bards who were so readily understood. And their message was that of loyalty to the Prince. Wales was the country of the squire and the peasant, but not of the merchant and trader. Parliament, the Welsh felt, favoured commercial classes and paid scant heed to the needs of those who lived on the land.

For these reasons, not only Wales, but also Scotland, Cumberland and Cornwall, which were all Celtic, gave their support to the King. In Parliament, with but few exceptions, the Welsh members were staunch royalists. They not only favoured the King in the House, but they also threw in their lot with him on the battlefield. It was on August 22nd, 1642, that King Charles unfurled his banner at Nottingham, and his first move was to Shrewsbury, there, as he said, "to sit down near the border of Wales where the power of Parliament has been least prevalent". It was a wise move. Wales responded as he had anticipated, more than 5,000 Welshmen flocking to his standard. Unfortunately, he was unable to supply them with arms, ammunition or even provisions.

The Civil War, which opened in 1642 with the Battle of Edgehill, may be divided into two main periods. The first ended with the King's flight to Scotland in 1646. The second period opened with his escape in November, 1647, and ended with his execution in January, 1649. But here we are concerned only with the part which Wales played in this great and tragic drama.

When King Charles went over to the offensive, he tried to take London, but failed to do so. In 1642 the royalists met with success when they captured Cardiff Castle under the leadership of Lord Herbert. His army was fitted out, maintained and even paid by his father, the Marquis of Worcester, an ancestor of the present Duke of Beaufort. This demonstrates the loyalty the King could command among the great land-owners. But the royalist cause was destined to meet reverses even in Wales. In 1643 the forces of Charles I were contained by the Parliamentary army which was based on Gloucester and commanded the Severn Valley. In the North, the parliamentary forces were also successful. They had the decisive advantage of artillery, an arm which the royalists wholly lacked. The points of resistance the monarchists were hoping to hold were overrun.

Wales, however, was taking a strong hand in preserving the cause of Charles. By the end of 1643, Welsh fighters were pinning down large Parliamentary forces which would otherwise have been free to operate against the royalist forces operating in England. But the initiative was not to remain in the hands of the monarchists. In the first months of 1644 a change took place in the course of the war which was to have fateful results for the royalists and, ultimately, fatal results for Charles I. The leadership of the Parliamentarians was taken out of the hands of men like the Earl of Essex because it was felt they were not prosecuting the war with sufficient vigour. New men appeared on the scene—Cromwell, Ireton and Harrison—men who were informed with the crusading fervour of the religious zealot. These men were not content to leave the initiative to the monarchist forces. They went over to the offensive.

In Wales, Lord Herbert attacked Pembroke with his private army, but without success. And Laugharne, a tough Roundhead, was prosecuting the war with a steady determination which slowly gained him control over South Wales. Using Irish forces, Gerard attempted to restore the situation. He might have succeeded, but his army was so lacking in discipline that it behaved like a rabble. They caused such deep and widespread resentment amongst the people that the Royalist cause completely lost the support of South Wales. By the end of the year, Monmouth and Brecon had fallen to Parliament.

In Chester, Prince Rupert, who was Count Palatine of the Rhine and Duke of Bavaria, had the title of President of Wales. The son of Frederick V of Bohemia and Elizabeth, daughter of James I of England, he served as general of the horse in the army of Charles I. It was to him that repeated appeals for help came from England, and he left North Wales in the care of Sir John Mennes, who was Governor of that part of the country. Unfortunately for the Royalist cause, the troops commanded by Prince Rupert were of a no more orderly disposition than those under the command of Gerard. Rupert's forces were severely defeated by Cromwell at Marston Moor, and the remnants of his army fled over the border to Wales. There they did further serious damage to Charles's cause by indulging in an orgy of pillaging. Such conduct alienated sympathy in the very regions where support for the King would otherwise have been very strong indeed. And the Roundheads were the kind of men to make the most of such a situation. In September, the Parliamentary forces routed the royalists at Montgomery.

In spite of these reverses, Charles's cause was by no means lost. In the early months of 1645, in Wales at least there was an improvement in the fortunes of the King. In the west, Gerard achieved some degree of success. But the political and military skill of the Roundheads was superior to that of the Royalists. A new Model Army was formed, and, in June, there occurred the Battle of Naseby, in which the King suffered a crushing defeat. The outcome had a special significance for Wales. Naseby was the last great pitched battle of the wars, and the Welsh made up the bulk of the royalist infantry. Thereafter, the exchanges between the two sides were limited to skirmishes and seiges, and in these Gerard had some success

King Charles now tried to raise another army, but he found his task virtually impossible. The people were so bitter on account of the treatment they had received from the dissolute troopers of Prince Rupert and Gerard, that there was but little willingness to join the royal ranks. The squires exerted their influence on behalf of the King, but with scant effect. The few recruits who joined, or who expressed a willingness to do so, demanded conditions of service. They insisted that Welshmen should fight under Welsh officers. And, remembering what had happened in the past, they also demanded that there must be no arrears of pay. The royalist authorities were also informed that soldiers were to be boarded on civilians for one night only. There was a new spirit of independence abroad, and it was to prove fatal for the royalists. At Raglan the King waited for an army that never arrived.

Events were taking a most ominous shape. In early 1646 Chester had been surrendered to the Roundheads. This had been followed by the failure of the King's cause at Raglan. Soon afterwards, only Harlech Castle remained in royalist hands. It was obvious that there could be no further appeal to arms. In April, 1646, King Charles surrendered to the Scottish army. The first Civil War was over. Nothing, however, had been finally resolved. In 1647 quarrels broke out between Parliament and the Army. In Wales the divisive influence was religion. The Welsh resented the triumph of the Army and the Independents, and there was some changing of sides. Roundheads like Laugharne, for instance, went over to the King.

The Parliamentary forces in Wales, however, were throwing up new leaders. One of these was Thomas Mytton of Halston, near Oswestry. This was the Mytton who was destined to have a most colourful and curious descendant in Jack Mytton. It was Jack Mytton who scandalised and amused the nineteenth century by his eccentric and extravagant behaviour. He was a sportsman and an outrageous spendthrift, and he astonished as well as appalled friends and acquaintances by setting fire to his clothes in order to end bouts of hiccups. Col. Thomas obviously had some of his spirit if none of his panache. He defeated Sir John Owen and so secured North Wales for Parliament.

The greatest of the Welsh Parliamentarians was undoubtedly Colonel John Jones, the Welsh regicide, who came from Merioneth. He was a man of rare courage, and one who was wholly committed to the Roundhead cause. He was married to Oliver Cromwell's sister, and shared with the Lord Protector the conviction that there could be no compromise with the King. The aim was complete victory for the Parliamentarians and unconditional surrender of the Royalists. He played a leading part in the organising of the new Model Army. For those who believe in the sanctity of monarchy his name remains an anathema. Eor it was Colonel John Jones who played a decisive part in condemning Charles I to the block. Not only did he sit in the court which condemned the King, but his was the hand that signed the royal death warrant. During the Commonwealth he occupied positions of considerable importance. He was a man of the rarest metal. When the monarchy was restored in 1660, he knew that he could expect the vengeful hand of Charles II to fall on him without mercy. He also knew that death would be the end of his punishment and not the beginning. He made no effort to escape from London. With a dignity that nothing could disturb, he faced his trial and suffered the appalling barbarities meted out to men adjudged to be traitors. The punishment had not changed since the execution of Dafydd, the brother of Llywelyn the Last. Jones suffered unspeakable cruelties, as did, of course, other Roundhead leaders.

But in November, 1647, King Charles I was still nominally the ruler of the country, and he precipitated the Second Civil War when he managed to escape from captivity. His freedom inspired his supporters in certain quarters, and, in February, 1648, Colonel Poyer, the Governor of Pembroke Castle, drove the Parliamentary forces out of the county. This sparked off a revolt on behalf of the Royalists which engulfed most of Wales. But the Parliamentarians were now committed to a ruthless crushing of all opposition. One of these most able leaders of the Roundheads, a man called Horton, was sent into the Principality in command of a strong force of the New Model Army. In May he defeated Laugharne at St. Fagans. But this was only the beginning of the defeat of the Principality. He was joined by no less a person than Oliver Cromwell himself. Cromwell was of Welsh descent, but he showed no reluctance to subjugate Wales. With Horton he set about the task in a ruthless and systematic manner. Their progress was marked by a trail of destruction. Some towns, such as Brecon, pulled down their walls to save the citizens from the attentions of Cromwell's Ironsides. Meanwhile, in North Wales, Thomas Mytton was completing his work. Pembroke Castle was taken, and the Civil War in Wales was at an end.

There began for Wales a far from happy period. During the Commonwealth, because of its royalist sympathies, the country fared badly. The Government refused to regard or treat the Principality as a separate country. Such treatment, of course, merely served to confirm the people in their beliefs, and the vast majority continued to be both royalist and episcopalian. The Puritans, as if determined to ensure the alienation of Welsh sympathy, sent Commissioners into the country to enforce the Act "for the propagation of the gospel in Wales". This was a course of conduct which aroused a great deal of resentment. The opposition to the Roundheads was led by men like Morgan Llwyd and Vavasor Powell. They preached the complete separation of the Church and State, demanded religious toleration and a form of democracy in which there was no place for an all powerful Protector.

In 1660 the monarchy was restored, and Charles II ascended the throne. The old order was re-established, and, as it was said at the time, "The squire dispensed justice, the parson preached loyalty, the bard in remote Nannau praised the life of Charles the First and bewailed his death, and the peasant was told the world was put right again". Once more it was a matter of business as usual. Again the gentry and merchants looked towards London, and the parochial way of life continued. But for known Parliamentarians there was persecution. Life was made so difficult for some Welsh people who had favoured the Roundheads that they decided to seek safety and a new life in America. In 1682 a large group left Bala, in Merioneth, to found a colony in Pennsylvania. There, as time went by, they were joined by other Welsh people. The settlement was given the name of Meirion because Meirion had been the home of Colonel John Jones and Morgan Llwyd. On the settlement rose the city of Philadelphia, which even today has strong Welsh connections.

Reminders of the Civil Wars and their savage courses can still be traced throughout Wales. In the graveyards Royalists and Roundheads lie together. Church doors still have marks where bullets bit into them, bullets fired by Cromwell's soldiers when executing Royalists.

The life of Charles I was by no means without its effect. He showed considerable courage when deprived of his throne, and he never lost a vestige of dignity when faced with a hostile Parliament. Even when he stood before the block, he betrayed no sign of fear. He might have displayed more poltical wisdom and perhaps greater resilience as a monarch, but he knew how a King should behave as a person and that was how he behaved. In many quarters he was thought of more highly after his death than during his life. But he also left behind more than a reput- ation. After suffering defeat at Rowton in 1645, the royalist army encamped near Llandrinio, where the King lodged in a house. His stay there resulted in the birth of a royal child who took the name of Prince.*

In 1714 the Elector of Hanover (George Ludwig), became King George I of England, and this resulted in a change in the position of Wales. The Welsh certainly favoured the Jacobite cause, and they were made to pay for supporting the House of Stuart. The instruments of power were not allowed to fall into their hands, and they had no authority either in the Church or in administering the law. The Welsh made evident their feelings about George I by rioting throughout their country when he assumed the crown. In 1715 there occurred the Jacobite rising by the Old Pretender, James Francis Edward Stuart, the son of James II. This was defeated at Preston and Sheriffmuir, and it had no effect on Wales. But one pleasing episode occurred during this futile rebellion. Lord Nithdale escaped from the Tower of London, and he did so because of the devoted efforts of his wife, who was Welsh.

It was a different matter, however, when the Young Pre- tender, Charles Edward Stuart, son of the Old Pretender, led his bid for the throne. The Welsh had quite a hand in that. Since the Jacobite rising of 1715 the Welsh bards had kept alive the memory of the "King over the water". Scotch firs which had been planted on the hillsides in his memory were a constant reminder of the Stuarts and their cause.

Throughout Wales there existed organisations committed to promoting Jacobite sympathy. One of these was known as the Cycle of the White Rose. This was a secret society drawn

---

*See Phillips, "Civil War in Wales and the Marches".

from the Welsh gentry, and in North Wales it was headed by
the powerful Sir Watkin William Wynn of Wynstay, an
influential member of Parliament. The Cycle, which was most
active in North Wales and the Marches, was in touch with
similar bodies throughout Wales. The Duke of Beaufort led
a similar organisation in South Wales.

In order to conceal his part in the activities against George II,
Sir Watkin used the code name Brutus, and it was under this
name that he corresponded with the Young Pretender, Prince
Charles. In 1744, Sir Watkin urged Prince Charles to make a
bid for the throne. He could hardly have done so had he not,
at the same time, assured him that he could be sure of significant
support from the people of Wales.

In 1745 the Young Pretender landed in Scotland, determined
to displace George II from the English throne. In Scotland he
met with considerable success and, on the 1st November, he
began to march southwards. He crossed into England, taking
Carlisle, and there he was met by two young Welshmen,
David Morgan of Tredegar and Robert Vaughan of Merioneth.
This must have seem to Charles confirmation of the support he
could expect from the Welsh. It appears, however, that he had
other evidence in the shape of messages from Sir Watkin. The
Prince was very short of cavalry. This was the kind of force
Sir Watkin could have raised, and it seems fair to conclude that
he had promised to furnish the Prince with the mounted troops
he needed. But there occurred one of those curious omissions
which are never satisfactorily explained and which occur
again and again throughout history. Prince Charles led his men
as far south as Derby. But his position was becoming more and
more precarious with every mile that he advanced. He needed
assurance that he was to receive the reinforcements without
which victory was bound to elude him. But there was no news
from Wales, and Charles had no alternative but to retreat. It
is said that Sir Watkin did, in fact, write a letter, but that it
arrived too late. Perhaps the Prince made a mistake in not
withdrawing into Wales. Had he done so things might have
turned out differently for him. A Welsh rebellion and Welsh
support might have made all the difference to the outcome of the
struggle. Men were on the march, intent on joining the Stuart

forces, but they turned back when Sir Watkin gave no lead. Why he failed to act at such a decisive moment has never been explained. There could hardly have been a personal quarrel with the Young Pretender, as Sir Watkin continued to correspond with him, and the members of the Cycle of the White Rose went on holding meetings. No doubt, the Government would have been pleased to lay hands on Sir Watkin, but he was too powerful for them to arrest him.

Had the Government dared to apprehend him, things must have gone badly for him. Proof of this seems to rest in the treatment meted out to David Morgan. He decided against following the Prince north. Instead, he tried to make his way back to Wales, but he was arrested at Stone, taken to London and executed as a traitor. Robert Vaughan was more fortunate. He fought at Culloden in 1746, where the forces of Prince Charles were defeated by the Duke of Cumberland. But he managed to escape capture and find sanctuary in Spain where he served in the Spanish court.

History is so much a matter of ' if ' that speculation as to what might have been is idle and fruitless. But it can be said with confidence that the whole course of Welsh history might well have been changed had Sir Watkin Williams Wynn given Prince Charles the military support he needed in those critical weeks of 1746.

XVI

HENRY MORGAN—BUCCANEER AND PATRIOT

1635—1688

'Twelve hundred rattling skeletons
Who sprang to life, and then
Like a wild wave took Panama
For they were Morgan's men.
—Henry Morgan's March on Panama,
PRYS-JONES.

ON advertisements hoardings throughout the British Isles there appears a figure sumptuously dressed in restoration costume, holding out a bottle of rum. This is Henry Morgan, the Welshman from Tredegar, the Pirate King. He pursued a career that must rank as one of the most colourful and adventurous in history, and he not only became a Knight, but he had what might well be the unique distinction of becoming an Admiral and a Colonel.

Like the posters which recall this buccaneer, everything Henry Morgan did was much larger than life. His exploits have become legendary, and his courage can hardly have been surpassed. But it was his vision and wisdom which explain the remarkable quality of his life. Had he been merely an adventurer, he would probably have been remembered—if at all—as no more than a pirate and an admirable rogue. But Henry Morgan was nothing less than an architect of British power in the Caribbean, and his achievements rank with those of Drake and Raleigh.

Henry Morgan was the son of a Welsh landowner, and was born at Tredegar, near Cardiff. He was descended from Sir John Morgan, who was a Knight of the Holy Sepulchre and connected with the great house of Tredegar, which could make the proud claim that it had provided Wardens of the Welsh Marches since the days of King Arthur. Henry Morgan came into the world in 1635, and for him that was hardly the most fortunate time. Before the Civil Wars, Wales had been royalist in sympathy, and it had been a land of laughter and revelry. But by the time Henry reached boyhood, Puritanism had spread its chill, inhibiting influence over Wales, creating an atmosphere that was by no means to his liking.

In Cardiff he saw the tall ships that crossed and recrossed the seas, and he listened to the tales (often taller than the ships) told by the sailors. But it was not the sea which attracted Henry. It was what lay beyond it, for this youth, who was to make his name as a buccaneer, was essentially a landsman. And when he left Cardiff, with nothing in his pocket but a few hard earned shillings, he did not put to sea. He merely crossed the channel to Bristol, where he went to work on the docks. But, in the evenings, he heard lurid tales of the Brethren of the Coast, and he heard them from men who were descendants of those who had sailed with such great heroes as Drake, Raleigh, Frobisher and Hawkins. He heard the alluring clinking of coins and his nostrils were invaded by the mixed smell of the ships' cargoes.

The Caribbean offered a tempting future to a lad like Henry Morgan, who was brimming with spirit and ambition. He signed on before the mast on a barque sailing for Jamaice, and if he didn't already know that life was bruisingly, even brutally tough, he must have learned the truth then. Floggings were common, and one can conclude that Henry had his share of this type of punishment. Conditions on board were atrocious by any standard, and the mortality rate amongst seamen of all types was disquietingly high. But however testing the initial voyage proved for Henry, worse was to come. The voyage ended in disaster, the ship failing to reach its destination. But whether it went down in a storm, or whether it was captured by pirates is not known. What is certain is that Henry survived, but while he saved his life, he lost his freedom. He was taken to Barbados where he was sold as a bondsman. This was as arduous a form of slavery as any other, the victims being indentured for many years, and to masters who were determined to get full value for the money they had laid out on their labour force.

Henry Morgan, however, was not one to endure the life of a bondsman. A born leader, he fomented a revolt and led a small party of fellow slaves to the coast. Courage and luck seem

to go hand in hand, and this was the case with Henry. He not
only found a boat, but one that was provisioned and ready to sail,
and so he and his fellows made the journey to Tortuga, off the
north-west coast of Hispaniola. And Tortuga had a great claim
to fame. It was the stronghold of the pirates, the Brethren of
the Coast.

On this island were gathered a cosmopolitan community
drawn from many races and bound together by an oath of
brotherhood. They were pirates and they regarded their calling
as strictly a business undertaking, and they ran it for large—
some would say huge—profits. It was inevitable that Henry,
who had such spirit, and whose taste of the world had been
bitter and abrasive, should join this brotherhood In 1659,
when he was still not twenty-five, he had his first blooding at the
sacking of St. Jago, a Spanish town in Hispaniola. It was a
great success and he, in common with all the other brethren,
received 300 doubloons as a ' keepsake of St. Jago '. He spent
the next few years mastering the tough arts and practices of the
buccaneer, taking part in raids on the coast of South America
and capturing prizes at sea.

It was during this period that he made a lifelong friend in
another Welshman, John Morris. Such were his qualities of
spirit and daring that, within five years, Henry Morgan was
elected Captain of his ship and he marked the event by leading
a raid on Campeche, in the state of Tucatan, Mexico. The
exploit was significant because Campeche was the treasure
house of Central America, and it was the kind of venture that
was to prove typical of the man throughout his piratical life.
It was hardly surprising that he said in later life, "I have been
more used to the pike than the book". But he mastered every
aspect of his trade as a pirate, despite his dislike of the sea. At
heart a soldier, he used the ocean merely as a highway to take
him to his objective, and he settled the issue by a land attack.

During Henry Morgan's years of apprenticeship to the
"sweet trade" of piracy, the Brethren had elected as Admiral of
the Black the tight-lipped, competent Dutchman, Edward
Mansfeld. Mansfeld, who understood men and their qualities,
had watched the young Welshman with growing appreciation.
He saw that here was a man who knew how to lead, and whose

courage was matched by a ruthless determination.   Perhaps because he saw that his own position would not be secure if Morgan decided to establish his own independent band, Mansfeld promoted him to the position of Vice Admiral of the Black, and he did that when Henry was only thirty years old !

The Brethren could now command a substantial fleet manned by the toughest sailors afloat, made up of Welsh, English, Dutch and French, supplemented by allies from inhabitants of the islands. Under the leadership of men like Mansfeld, who was prudent and calculating, and Henry Morgan, who was daring to the point of being over-bold, it was evident to the Governor of Jamaica—at that time the far-seeing Modyford— that the energies of such a force should be harnessed to ensure the safety of the islands, for his own protection and for his country's profit.

In 1665 Henry Morgan was in command of a small fleet of pirate ships based on Tortuga. In that same year Governor Modyford was joined by Colonel Edward Morgan as Deputy Governor of Jamaica. The Colonel was a royalist who had been exiled by Cromwell. He was Henry's uncle and was soon to be his father-in-law. In 1666 Governor Modyford took a decision which was to alter the history of the British Caribbean. By a letter of marque* the pirates ceased to be buccaneers and became privateers, charged with the duty of serving "England's purpose in the Caribbean against whatever country she might be at war with—or felt undisposed to". This curious transformation resulted in the Jolly Roger being replaced at the masthead by the highly respectable, even highly honourable Cross of St. George. The privateers moved their headquarters to Port Royal. And Henry Morgan entered into the second phase of his astounding career.

During the next few years the privateers undertook so many exploits and with such success that the Spaniards said of them "such conquests would soon enable them to become masters of all these countries". A new phrase was heard in the Caribbean Seas, "That is Harry Morgan's way", and it became a byword.

---

*A licence granted by one state to make reprisals at sea on the subjects of another state.

In 1667 Edward Mansfeld died, and Henry Morgan was unanimously elected as Admiral in Chief of the Brethren of the Coast. He had achieved this position at the astonishingly early age of thirty-two, and he was at the height of his powers. He had amassed a fortune, and his wife lived on the Morgan estate— a large one—in Jamaica. But Government House had received disquieting news. It was said that the Spaniards were preparing to seize Jamaica, and Morgan was summoned to discuss the situation with the Governor. And it was in this situation that Morgan acquired the title of Colonel. Not only was he given a commission as Colonel Henry Morgan, but he was also given "a free hand with men and ships against the Spaniards". He was empowered to take whatever action he felt the situation required. Being Morgan, he took action that was to prove decisive. The richest prize in the Caribbean was Havana, and second to it was Puerto Principe, which was strongly defended. Morgan attacked Principe and took it, doing so quickly and expeditiously. It was a hint that was not lost on the Spaniards. Jamaica was secure.

Henry Morgan, however, had too restless a spirit to pursue a peaceful existence. He longed for and looked for other prizes. On the Atlantic coast of Central America was the city of Puerto Bello, which ranked second only to Panama for riches. It offered a challenge, and the strongest Morgan had ever faced. Puerto Bello had defied Drake, and it was regarded as impregnable from attack made by sea. Which explains why Colonel Morgan decided to make his assault by land. It was an almost reckless exploit, and so much so that some of his men suggested they had not sufficient numbers to undertake such a project. He retorted with words which displayed the spirit of Harry of Monmouth on the eve of Agincourt, and which have clear echo in the sea shanty :

> ' If few there be among us,
>   Our hearts are very great,
>   And each will have more plunder,
>   And each will have more plate '.

Puerto Bello fell. But that was not all. Harry Morgan gave notice to the Spanish Governor that he intended to return to take Panama.

It was a bold promise to make, and the Spaniards could hardly have thought that he would keep it. Panama was the link between the Spanish colonies and Madrid. It was the market and principal city of the Spanish main, and it linked the two oceans. It was a prize beyond the dreams of any pirate—except Henry Morgan. It was, of course, heavily defended and was not readily accessible. To reach it a march had to be made across the isthmus from sea to sea, a march that involved carrying considerable weapons and supplies. If Henry Morgan had anything in his favour, it was limited to his own dauntless courage, and the spirit he was able to inspire in his men.

In 1667 a peace treaty had been signed between England and Spain, but in this agreement to end hostilities there had been no mention of ships. In any case, a ' mere piece of paper ' could hardly be allowed to hinder the aims of either side. Nevertheless, the agreement had been freely negotiated, and there had to be a show of honouring it. To ease the conscience of Whitehall— always elastic when trade and empire were involved—Modyford in his dispatches listed the towns sacked by his privateers as ships. Everybody was satisfied, except, of course, the Spaniards. Modyford, in fact, skilfully acted as a buffer between a Government which, officially, was seeking to appease the Spaniards, but which also needed the offensive action to be taken which would consolidate British power in the Caribbean.

For a time Henry Morgan had to be content with looking after his estates. But not quite. All the time he was preparing the expedition to Panama. The taking of this city, he knew, would set the seal on his career as a privateer, and he was determined not to be disappointed. At Port Royal there was activity of the kind never seen there before. Arms, ammunition and ships were being made ready, and men were being trained for the varied tasks the expedition involved. But naked aggression was undesirable. The assault, when it came, had to have some sort of justification. And, in June 1670, the Spaniards provided Modyford and Morgan with the excuse they needed. Some Spaniards made a raid on the shores of Jamaica.

Modyford responded to this act of offence instantly. He appointed Henry Morgan Admiral of the White and Commander in Chief of all ships of war in Port Royal. His terms of reference—worded with the greatest possible care—were to attack any vessels and to make such landings as might be required "to tend to the preservation and quiet of the island". The two men understood each other perfectly. Admiral Morgan had been given a free hand.

There was, however, not a moment to lose. While the final details for the assault on Panama were being completed with all possible speed, ships were on their way across the Atlantic bringing details of a definite peace treaty concluded between England and Spain. The Governor had orders to ensure that the privateer obeyed these instructions. Officially, Modyford sent the necessary orders, but so timing their despatch that they were bound to arrive too late. Unofficially, one may assume that he had advised Morgan to sail before they arrived.

The expedition to Panama was much more than Harry Morgan's greatest exploit. It was also an historical event. Its outcome was to mean much to England for hundreds of years. It involved a pitched battle between regular armies in the open, and it was fought on Spanish-American territories. Morgan did not act as a buccaneer. As Admiral and Commander in Chief, he sailed under the White Ensign.

To secure his rear he captured Old Providence and San Lorenzo, the huge castle at the mouth of the river Chagres, which led across the isthmus. On 8th January, 1671, the expedition began the up river journey. For three days, due to brilliant seamanship, the fleet managed to make their way by water, overcoming numerous obstacles. At last, faced by a barrier of tree trunks, Morgan admitted that they must cover the rest of their journey by land He left a party to guard the ships, and, at the head of 1,200 men, he thrust his way into the jungle and into history. The progress of the force was watched by Indian scouts, who must have thought these men were out of their minds To anyone knowing the circumstances and the intentions prompting the undertaking, it must have seemed that Morgan and his men were attempting the impossible. The men had not been trained in the hazards and problems of jungle warfare, and everything they needed they had to carry. With a well blended mixture of jests and oaths, the Welshman inspired and heartened his men. They needed every encouragement, for they were being asked to undertake a gargantuan task in the most hostile circumstances.

Eventually they reached Venta de Cruce. There the jungle gave place to the cobbled highway which led to the Pacific. The journey had taken five days on a starvation diet while they marched through appalling country. Ahead lay Panama City. A halt was called when they were just outside the range of the guns. The attack was launched on the 18th of January. In three groups, arranged in diamond formation and under the leadership of John Morris, the 1200 men moved forward. In desperate efforts to break up the advance, the Spaniards used everything against the British, including herds of bulls and oxen. But Morgan's men had come too far and endured too much to be denied their prize now. Within two hours, the city of Panama was taken. But the Spaniards had set fire to the buildings and, by midnight, all that remained of the once proud habitation was a smoking ruin.

Morgan's men, however, were not perturbed. Gold and jewels did not burn, and Panama was to provide rich rewards for its conquerors. The privateers were experts at ' persuading ' people to reveal where their valuables were hidden. Morgan installed himself in the Governor's Palace and began an unsuccessful campaign to win the heart of a lovely Spanish lady. Meanwhile, his men were engaged on the pleasant business of systematic looting. By mid-February the City of Panama had been stripped of all its valuables, and Morgan's men moved to San Lorenzo where the loot was shared out. But the undertaking was not completed without disputes and quarrels. Nevertheless, when Henry Morgan arrived back at Port Royal, he did so with five ships heavily laden with treasure.

At Port Royal he was received as a conqueror, but it was obvious that his days with the Brethren of the Coast were at an end. The Spaniards were incensed by the sack of Panama, and it was essential to take steps to appease them. A scapegoat was needed, and Modyford was singled out to fill the role. He was charged with having failed to prevent Morgan undertaking his escapade, and he was recalled. But officialdom, like Morgan himself, was well satisfied. The Caribbean was now secure for England, a matter of the utmost importance.

When, in January, 1672, Morgan was ordered to return to London, "To answer for his offences against the King, his crown and dignity", he went without any feelings of alarm. This was the usual practice in such circumstances, and he was sure he had nothing to fear. In this he was proved right. For three years he remained in London, "awaiting the King's pleasure". An extremely wealthy man, he spent his time exploring the pleasures London had to offer. And, in Restoration London, this was plenty. He was lionized by the Court. There he met Louise de Kerouaville, Duchess of Portsmouth and King Charles's mistress. He also met the enchanting Nell Gwynne who, to avoid being mistaken for her hated rival, Louise, explained to the crowd, "Good people, I am the Protestant whore".

French wines and the climate ruined Henry Morgan's health, which declined for lack of sun and rum. But he made a lifelong friend in the young, gay and gallant Duke of Albermarle, son of the sober George Monk, who could claim the credit for restoring Charles II to the throne. The Duke was only 19, while Henry was almost twice his age, but each had much to offer to the other.

Inevitably, his nature being what it was, Henry Morgan wearied of the life London had to offer. He demanded that his case should be heard, and his request was granted. But the trial seems to have been an odd one, to say the least. The court, if such it can be called, was held in a state room in the Palace, and was limited to an audience between the King and Morgan, in the presence of the Spanish Ambassador.

For Morgan, the case was simplicity itself. In his defence he limited himself to referring to the terms of his commission from the Port Royal Council. He denied all knowledge of orders which would have prevented him from sailing, and he explained that he had destroyed Panama because its wealth and guns were a threat to England. The Spanish Ambassador made the point that offiicialdom in Panama had warned Morgan that Spain and England were at peace. This brought a grin to the Welshman's face. Looking at the King, he observed blandly that he could not remember receiving any such warning, but that even if he had, how could he be expected to pay attention ? As everybody knew, the Spaniards could lie the sun out of heaven !

King Charles roared with laughter. As he had foreseen must be the case, Henry Morgan was adjudged guiltless, and, on 20th November, 1673, he was made a knight. In January, the following year, he received the King's commission to serve as Lieutenant Governor of Jamaica. In 1675 he returned to Jamaice with his friend Modyford, who had been appointed Chief Justice of the Island. But the new Governor of Jamaica was a man called Vaughan. This was unfortunate, as Morgan and Vaughan disliked each other. While Vaughan occupied himself on the island, Henry Morgan ruled in Port Royal, where he pursued his policy of encouraging privateers—and pirates. He had the wisdom to see that England's real enemy was no longer Spain, but France, and he directed his aims accordingly. Vaughan did not approve of Morgan's plans, but he was powerless to command his popular Lieutenant. Eventually he was recalled and his successor was Lord Carlisle, an old friend of Henry's. They were former drinking companions, both were Royalists and shared similar interests. But there was one difference between the two men which had been overlooked in London. Morgan was a Jamaican patriot, while Carlisle was a British imperialist.

Due to Morgan's activities, Jamaica was very rich, and had enough wealth to make it independent. Morgan told the Governor bluntly that the Jamaican Assembly would never accept Whitehall's proposal that its powers should be limited to merely ratifying, and not to making or rejecting laws. Morgan, in fact, was aiming to see the island achieve dominion status. Carlisle could not agree. He tried without success to impose his policies on the Assembly. Realising he was destined only to suffer frustration, he resigned. Thus he made way for a new Governor, and the appointment was given to Sir Henry Morgan, himself.

By this time—1680—Sir Henry was living a highly respectable life, and he now turned his attention to piracy. He opposed the crime with such vigour that, within a year, he had almost destroyed the Brotherhood he had once led with such skill. But, in 1682, a new governor was appointed, and this was none other than one of Morgan's old enemies, a man named Lynch.

Supported by Whitehall, he relieved Sir Henry of his appointment as Acting Governor of Jamaica. In October, the following
year, Sir Henry suffered an even greater indignity. The
Assembly stripped him of all his offices and commands. With no
public work to engage him, Sir Henry busied himself on his
estate, indulging in the fascinating sport of litigation, in which he
won a libel suit. But his attention was chiefly drawn to the
possibilities of discovering at least some of the treasure which
had been sunk and buried on the Spanish main. In this highly
speculative field he could be regarded as the foremost expert.

During this time he was in touch with the Duke of
Albemarle, who shared his interest. And, in 1686, Sir Henry's
fortunes took a distinct turn for the better. In the September of
that year, Albemarle succeeded in having himself made Governor
of Jamaica, and armed with wide powers to organise treasure
hunting. It was a happy reunion between the old friends, and
Albemarle's first step was to restore Sir Henry to his seat on the
Council. It was also his intention to make him once more
Lieutenant Governor of the island. With the enthusiasm of
schoolboys, they planned to hunt for treasure on a grand scale.
But there was to be no such undertaking for Sir Henry. He
knew he had not long to live. In 1678 he had been given a
charm of the Bezoar of a white ape which, he had been assured,
would protect him for ten years. Not only was that decade
expiring, but, on Good Friday, 1688, a Judas gum dripped red
on a woman famed as being ' wise '. According to Jamaican
legend, the tree bleeds in memory of the crucifixion, and that
when it does so it foretells that a great soul will soon be on its
way to heaven. Whatever the truth in the legend, to the
Jamaicans, Sir Henry Morgan was a great soul, and he did, in
fact, die on the 25th August, 1688. With him when he died
were his wife and his personal physician. When the doctor
refused to allow him his customary glass of rum, Sir Henry
exclaimed indignantly that he intended to enjoy death as he had
enjoyed every adventure while living, Sir Henry was given a
state funeral at Port Royal.

He was not, however, to be allowed to remain where human
hands had placed him. At the beginning of the eighteenth
century an earthquake shattered Port Royal. Along with the

old city the cemetery sank into the sea. And so the Admiral of the Black, the Colonel and Admiral of the White, returned to the Caribbean Sea.

Because of their romantic nature, Sir Henry Morgan's exploits as a pirate are remembered more than the far more important fact that he was the architect of the British Caribbean. It is also largely forgotten that he was the democrat who won for his island the first modern Constitution conceded to a colonial parliament. Because of his courage, his skill, his foresight and his personality, Sir Henry Morgan ranks with those foremost figures, Drake and Raleigh. He was, indeed, a great man and, of course, a great Welshman. Edward Long did not exaggerate when, in 1774, he wrote :

"Sir Henry Morgan, whose achievements are well known, was equal to any of the most renowned warriors of historical fame, in valour, conduct and success . . ."

XVII

JEMIMA AND THE BLACK LEGION

THE FISHGUARD INVASION OF 1797

Towards the end of 1796 there was planned an invasion of Britain which must rank as the most strange in history. It might, too, have had the most serious consequences.

The French Directory ordered a young fire-eater, a General named Lazare Hoche, to make a nuisance raid on the British Isles. It was to serve as a "curtain raiser" to a full-scale invasion. But its immediate aim was that of encouraging the poor to rise against their monarch, George III. This being the purpose, the French chose the most unlikely means to achieve it.

The men who were to carry out this coup were convicts from the gaols of Brest, and a more blood-thirsty, undisciplined and disreputable body it would be hard to imagine. Nor were their officers better than offscourings of the French Army, being described by their commanders as "undesirable". As for their commander, he was none other than Colonel Tate, an Irish-American who shared with Hoche a hatred for the English that was nothing less than pathological. Tate had a reputation as a rapist and murderer.

This strange and, apparently, terrifying body of men was rightly known as the Black Legion, and they were charged with the task of burning to ashes the city of Bristol. They were also to sail to Wales, march across the mountains and fall upon Chester and Liverpool. The men must have set out as eagerly as on a honeymoon. For their services they were to be pardoned for their crimes, they could pillage and plunder to the limits of their strength and opportunity, and all the women who fell into their hands were to be used in whatever way the convicts desired.

Tate was assured that the people of Wales so hated the English, they would flock to the French standard and fling themselves into the Revolution. And so, in high expectations, these cargoes of criminals sailed from Brittany on the 17th

February, 1797, escorted by the frigates 'Vengeance' and
'Resistance'.   Disguised in British uniforms, they carried
enough "combustible matter" to set fire to almost all the major
cities of the British Isles.

The Russian flag was hoisted off Land's End, and, under its
protection, the invaders entered the Bristol Channel, where
they were brought to a halt by an adverse wind   A party was
landed off Ilfracombe, and isolated farms were looted and
burned.   But, learning that the North Devon Volunteers were
on the march, the invaders returned to their vessels in some
disarray.   Anchor was hurriedly weighed and the journey to the
Welsh coast was resumed.

Tate, a man cursed with strange ideas, had kept all his
convicts on very thin rations, believing that this would increase
their martial spirit as well as their appetites.   His aim was to
ensure that his men were in a ferocious and ravenous mood.

Reaching St. David's Head on February 22nd, they landed
near the village of Fishguard in the early hours of the following
day.   In their famished state, they lost no time in ransacking
farms for food.   They washed down the eatables with large
draughts of wine, which the farmers had taken as 'treasure
trove' from a wrecked vessel.

Enraged and frightened by this treatment, the people hurriedly loaded carts with necessities and hastened inland, leaving the
French to spend the day looting and drinking.   The fleeing
families spread news of the invasion, and the French lost the
invaluable advantage of surprise.

Thomas Knox, Commander of the Fishguard Fencibles,
was at a dance at Tregwynt, near where the French had landed.
Learning of the invasion, he went to investigate, but he failed
to visit the cliffs, from which the French ships were visible.
Satisfied the reports of danger were false, he went on to Fishguard.   At Goodwick Sands he came upon seventy Fencibles
moving up to repel the invaders, and he ordered them to retire
to their fort at Lower Fishguard.

As the day wore on more men gathered to protect the coast,
while the Fencibles, though still not in contact with the enemy,
began to fall back on Haverfordwest.   Luckily, the civilians were
in a more militant mood than the soldiers who should have been

protecting them. A party of seamen from Solva attacked the intruders.

It was a woman, however, who was most prominent in the defence of the country. This was Jemima Nicholas, a cobbler woman of Fishguard. She earned undying fame by setting about the French with a pitchfork and in such a determined manner that she took several prisoners.

The wine, too, played a disarming role. Several hundred Legionaires became drunk and deserted.

Meanwhile, Lord Cawdor of Stackpole, Colonel of the Castle Martin Yeomanry, rounded up some of his men and marched north to meet the enemy. On the way he gathered in more men, including the retreating Fencibles.

Reaching the French outposts on the evening of February 28th, he deployed his men on the heights above Goodwick Sands. Although his force was barely half that of the enemy, he decided to attack. A body of spectators was provided by the Welsh women in their red cloaks and tall hats. No doubt encouraged by Jemima Nicholas, they had armed themselves with pokers, pitchforks and similar weapons.

The French commander now made two mistakes. In the dusk he took the watching women to be reinforcements. And when Cawdor decided to delay the attack until dawn and his drums sounded the retreat, Tate thought they signalled an assault and he ordered his men to retire. They did so, firing wildly as they went. French morale was low. The men had eaten and drunk to excess and were suffering from a king size hangover. Their supporting frigates had sailed away, and the British seemed to have overwhelming numbers. Tate sent officers to ask for terms. But Cawdor, although the odds were against him, demanded unconditional surrender.

Tate capitulated. The Black Legion surrendered their weapons on Goodwick Sands, watched by Jemima and her red-cloaked women. But they were not content to remain spectators. They made fierce attempts to get at the invaders, intent on cutting their throats.

The invasion convinced the people of Britain that the French, from Napoleon downwards, were nothing better than a besotted body of cowardly criminals, capable only of burning

barns and stealing chickens. But this relatively trifling incident
had sensational results. It created such a serious financial panic
that Britain came within hours of bankruptcy. The Government was forced to agree to a suspension of payments in gold
and other metals and, for the first time, the Bank of England
began to issue paper notes as legal tender. This was to prove of
immense economic value.* But more valuable perhaps was the
stupid experiment the French had made. Its failure inspired the
greatly needed feeling that Bonaparte was not invincible—an
attitude that was of crucial importance in the years ahead.

The Pembrokeshire Yeomanry carry the name ' Fishguard '
on their badge. The standard carried against the Black Legion is
preserved at Penpont, near Brecon. As for the redoubtable
Jemima, there is no record that she received any reward. But
she certainly had the satisfaction of knowing that she had not
hesitated to fight for her home and country when the French
had dared to invade land which she rightly regarded as sacred.

---

*In London a wit observed, "The Bank of England is much indebted
to the French for the Experiment."

XVIII

EISTEDDFODAU

' This innocent, peaceful strife,
This struggle to fuller life
Is still the one delight of Cymric souls—
Swell, blended rhythm ! still
The gay pavilions fill.
Soar, oh young voices, resonant and fair ;
Still let the sheathed sword gleam
           above the bardic chair '.
           ' At the Eisteddfod ' SIR LEWIS MORRIS.

THE Eisteddfod gives expression to the Welsh spirit. It is also a link with, as well as a reminder of a past that every Welshman is proud to celebrate. The competitions follow the same pattern a- the ceremonies which must have been held in the courts of the Welsh Princes, where the bard held a position of great importance. That Eisteddfodau are presented in Welsh in no way limits their appeal. Visitors need have no fear that ignorance of the language will spoil the enjoyment of either a na†ional or local Eisteddfod.

Experts, who have busied themselves consulting dusty tomes on half forgotten library shelves, claim that it is a fallacy to imagine that the ceremonies of the Eisteddfodau go back to ancient times. And it must be admitted that the modern National Eisteddfod originated at Llangollen in 1858. But the tradition of the Eisteddfodau can be traced back to the Druids of the pre-Roman era. It was they who established the ritual of dress, mistletoe, laurels and circle of stones. And they must have handed on, at least orally, their learning and customs.

Iolo Morganwg, who sometimes exalted fiction to the higher rank of fact, was not always a traitor to truth. It is certain that he drew his ideas from what he had learned of the Druids, and no one denies that the Gorsedd of the Bards, the Logan Stone and the Bardic Chair were real long before Iolo wrote at Primrose Hill. There is, undeniably, a continuity with the

great gatherings of the past, and the Eisteddfod is an integral
part of Welsh history.

During the Roman occupation the Druids preserved their
love of culture. There are records of Eisteddfodau held in the
Dark Ages. In 517 A.D., Taliesin, the Welsh poet, organised
one at Ystym Llwydiarth, and in 540 A.D. one was held on the
banks of the River Conway. It was typical of Welsh appreciation of the arts that Howell the Good made provision for a
place of honour to be reserved for the bard at Court. And it was
typical of the Welsh spirit that the bard was selected in open
competition. It is well known that the Princes of Gwynedd
were great patrons of culture, and history has not overlooked
the fact that, in 1176, Lord Rhys of Deheubarth was president
of the Cardigan Eisteddfod, which attracted competitors from
England and Scotland, as well as from all parts of Wales. One
of the competitors was the poet-prince Owain, a brother of
Madoc the explorer and an uncle of Llywelyn the Great.

Throughout the Middle Ages Eisteddfodau were an integral
part of Welsh life. At the Carmarthen Eisteddfod of 1451 it
was men from Flint who carried off all the prizes. This under-
lines the fact that national unity was achieved at the Eisteddfod,
the north and south meeting together in friendly rivalry. When
the Tudors ascended the throne of England it was only natural
that things Welsh should come very much into vogue. Bards
flourished. The Eisteddfodau enjoyed royal patronage, and in
1523 Henry VIII issued a commission, and Queen Elizabeth I
did the same thing in 1568. These gatherings were designed to
decide who were the most deserving of the travelling bards,
and those who were chosen received official licence. There is
abundant evidence to show that the Eisteddfodau have deep and
very distant origins.

The Methodist Revival evoked a new interest in Welsh
culture. In 1789 at Corwen, the Gorsedd of the Bards gave
permission for the public to be present for the first time. This
proved so successful that it was repeated at Bala that same year.

During the second half of the nineteenth century societies
came into being expressly to promote interest in the Welsh
language and culture. Each society sought to achieve its
purpose by promoting Eisteddfodau in the ancient divisions of

Wales and these were enthusiastically supported by the local people. Today similar assemblies attract the same degree of attention. In many countries overseas, as well as in England, there are flourishing Welsh societies. One of these, the Honourable Society of Cymrodorion, which has its headquarters in London, ranks among the foremost of these organisations, and has made a unique contribution to the task of preserving the Welsh language and promoting an understanding of Welsh history.

At Abergavenny, in 1838, a team from Brittany competed for the first time, and today the Bretons are regular visitors to the National Eisteddfod. The Bretons and Cornish are reminders of the close ties that exist between the Celtic races and which find a common link in King Arthur.

The National Eisteddfod is held annually during the first week in August, and since 1860 it has been held alternately in North and South Wales. The town selected for the venue is well aware that it has been greatly honoured.

The chief aim of Eisteddfodau is to keep alive Welsh culture and the Welsh language, and in this they certainly succeed. They also express the unity of a country which was rich in culture and romance long before Duke William cast covetous eyes across the sea from Normandy. What is regarded as of equal importance, they serve to cement the ties which exist with the Welshmen who lived abroad. They give expression to the British love of pageantry and ceremony, and they serve to keep alive a love of poetry, for the greatest honour is reserved for an ode and for a poem. For the winner there is the bardic chair, a purple robe and a wreath of laurels.

The white worn by the Archdruid symbolises the search for unsullied truth. He is distinguished by his gold collar and chaplet of oak leaves. He presides over the Gorsedd of the Bards, which ranks as one of the most important sections of the National Eisteddfod Council, and he has the help of various officers, among them the Herald Bard and the Sword Bearer. The Gorsedd consists of three orders. The ovates, who wear green, which signifies they are novitiates ; the previous Archdruid and Druids, who appear in gleaming white, as does the acting Archdruid, and there is, of course, the Bard, who is robed in sky blue, which denotes heavenly light.

The blade of the Grand Sword is lavishly engraved, and the crystal in its hilt represents mystery. On the scabbard—wooden to signify peace—are the mottoes of the five ancient provinces of Wales—Morgannwg (Glamorgan), Gwent, Gwynedd, Powys and Dyfed. The Banner of the Gorsedd shows a dragon in the centre of a blazing sun, encircled by the Gorsedd motto, "The Truth Against The World". A symbol which attracts great attention is the Hirlas Horn. Ornamented with the design of a dragon and a druid with a harp, when not in use it rests on a magnificent silver dragon which holds a large crystal in its claws.

The split sword symbolises the unity that exists between Wales and Brittany, and it was a gift from Brittany in 1899. While the Welsh half carries a design of leeks and a dragon, the Breton half displays the arms of Duchess Anne of Brittany. All the regalia can be seen in the National Museum of Wales in Cardiff during the fifty-one weeks that separate the Eisteddfodau.

Throughout the week there are ceremonies which can only have their roots in the past. The offerings of mead and honey, for instance, of fruits and flowers, the traditional singing and recitations are the products of an ancient tradition. Certainly the setting of the ceremonies within a circle of stones in the face of the sun, ' the eye of light ', goes back so far that its origin is lost in the thick folds of time.

Her Majesty, Queen Elizabeth, was invested as an ovate at the Mountain Ash Eisteddfod in 1936. Her parents had been admitted to the Bardic circle at Swansea in 1926.

Wales is pre-eminently a land of song and romance. It is this tradition which the Eisteddfodau help to keep alive. It is a worthy expression of nationalism—the kind of nationalism that can only serve to extend friendship and understanding between nations.

XIX

DAVID LLOYD GEORGE
THE WELSH WIZARD
1863—1945

*' His tenor voice was admirable : musical, beautifully
modulated, and of remarkable carrying power '—(comparison
with Gladstone)—' its compass was narrower, its quality
lighter, it was flexible, caressing, a melodious witchery, mockery,
savagery . . . He played on all the strings of the human heart
and matched with each the mobile landscape of his face and
bodily posture—the alluring smile, the scowling visage, the
thrilling whisper, the eloquent pince-nez dangling from its
black silk ribbon, the menacing finger, the arms outstretched
to the uttermost '.*

—*Lloyd George*, DR. THOMAS JONES.

DAVID LLOYD GEORGE stands, without question, as the foremost
Welshman of his day. His achievements were numerous,
varied and, in some instances, of decisive national and international significance. He was the architect of the Allied
victory in World War One. Along with his great friend
Winston Churchill, he was the founder of the National Insur-
ance Scheme which, taken for granted today, was won only as
the result of immense effort and in face of large and obdurate
opposition. His Budget of 1911 contained egalitarian measures
which heralded the beginning of the end of ' The Two Nations '
so vividly described by Disraeli, and led to the drastic curbing
of the powers of the House of Lords. He fought for, and
achieved, the disestablishment of the Welsh Church, and he
formed the basis of some degree of independent government for
Wales.

He was to achieve the highest temporal position, but he
never lost sight of his Welsh origins, and his love for Wales, its
people and its countryside remained a paramount influence to the
last. He will always be remembered as the epitome of the proud
spirit which informs his countrymen, and his name will for long

conjure the mystery and romance of Wales—a quality he shared with Owen Glendower. It was his Welsh background and upbringing which turned the penniless lawyer into a world statesman, and transformed the barnstorming radical into one of the greatest orators of his day and the undisputed master of the House of Commons.

His radical political philosophy and his great social and political achievements have their inspiration in his boyhood days, when class was more important than talent or ability. It was the era which prompted the famous couplet,

' *God bless the squire and his relations*
   And keep us in our proper stations ',

which was not only quoted by the conventional with sincerity, but by the radicals with irony. David Lloyd George was, in fact, the son of a schoolmaster, but amongst his relations he had an uncle who was a cobbler, and in those days that meant poverty of a harsh, if not extreme, kind.

Lloyd George, as the world came to know him, was not born in Wales. His parents chose for him the damp, industrially tainted air of Manchester for his birth place, and there he entered the world on January 17th, 1863. His father came of good yeomen stock, having originated in Fishguard, in Pembrokeshire. His paternal grandmother may well have been one of Jemima Nicholas's followers and helped to route Napoleon's Black Legion in 1797. His mother, from whom he gained his Christian name, was Elizabeth Lloyd of a North Wales family, the Lloyds of Llwyndyrus. They could claim connections with Sir Gryffud Lloyd and the astronomer, Richard Lloyd. His uncle was another Richard Lloyd. This last fact has a clear historical echo. Henry Tudor owed a great debt to his uncle, Jasper Tudor, and Lloyd George was glad to acknowledge that he owed much to his uncle, Richard Lloyd.

When David was a year old, his father abandoned his career as a schoolmaster and returned to his home-land, taking over a smallholding near Haverfordwest. It might have been health reasons which prompted this change, for he died the following year. It was at this point that David's uncle, Richard Lloyd, accepted responsibility for the young, fatherless family. He took them to his home in the village of Llanystumdwy, which lies in

the shadow of the mighty Snowdonian range and overlooks
Caernarvon Bay. It was there that Lloyd George took in the
romance of Wales with every breath he drew. And, no matter
where duty and fame might take him, he retained an unbroken
affection for the district. In later years, when he was a world
figure, it was always to Criccieth that he returned. The heart of
every Welshman is in Wales, but none more so than was the
heart of Lloyd George.

He owed much to Richard Lloyd because of what his uncle
was. He was the ideal guide and mentor for a boy of David's
disposition. He was much more than a village cobbler. Richard
Lloyd's father had been a master cobbler, a true craftsman. But
he had also been a man of letters, a poet and local secretary of the
Cymmrodorion. Intelligent and studious, as well as a radical,
Richard Lloyd served as the unpaid minister of the Nonconformist Chapel. Of a sturdy independence of spirit, he was the
acknowledged leader of the community in the struggle between
the poor and the squirearchy. Like England and Scotland,
Welsh rural areas in those days tended to remain feudal.

Richard Lloyd inspired in his nephew's responsive heart and
mind a passion for learning, a love of the Welsh traditions and
an unflagging determination to champion the oppressed. The
stern old Puritan and the eager child were devoted to each
other. It was affection that prompted David to call him ' Esgob '
—the Bishop.

The young boy also learned the Celtic art of bringing imagination and artistry into his dealings with the minds of men.
He was to become noted for his superlative powers of persuasion
and for his ability to so anger his opponents that they were too
disturbed to properly formulate their case. He learnt with the
ease of the youth who is eager to know. Even as a boy in the
village school he imbibed knowledge readily and found time to
indulge his high spirits and sense of fun. He was a born leader
and dare-devil, as his whole life revealed. When any untoward
incident occurred in the village there was the almost inevitable
explanation, "It's that David Lloyd at it again !"

His uncle was quick to recognise the rare and many qualities
possessed by his nephew. He believed in him so unquestioningly
that he decided to make the great personal sacrifice of devoting

to him his life savings that he might have his chance in the world. This act of virtually unlimited generosity made it possible for Lloyd George to study law. He did so to such effect that, at the age of twenty-one, David Lloyd George presented himself to the world as a solicitor. He was penniless, but he had immense capital in his self-confidence and in his manifold gifts. He displayed his brass plate, announcing his name and profession, and he had soon built for himself a reputation for being a shrewd lawyer and one who took up with enthusiasm any case that he was offered. He was not hampered by any sense of false deference to the bench, any more than, later in life, he was to be overawed by the House of Commons. He was not to be browbeaten by any man or group of men, no matter how important they thought themselves to be.

Lloyd George's legal clients in those days were chiefly small farmers and shopkeepers. The poachers not only found him able in presenting their cases before the magistrates, but they also found that he was sympathetic to them. It was also obvious that he was hostile to the bench, which was composed almost exclusively of local landowners.

On one occasion Lloyd George presented the plea that the Court, made up wholly of landowners, had no jurisdiction in a poaching offence, due to the fact that they were interested parties. The Chairman told him that such a point should be decided by a higher court. This was a threat that in no way intimidated Lloyd George. He not only agreed, but added, "Yes, sir, in a perfectly just and unbiased court". The Chairman, taken aback, complained, "A more insulting and ungentlemanly remark to the bench I have never heard during my experience as a magistrate". Not at all abashed, Lloyd George replied tartly, "Yes, and a more true remark was never made in a Court of Justice". The point was taken. The bench knew that it had taken a caning.

By the time he was twenty-five, Lloyd George had made for himself a local reputation as an advocate. And it was the case of an old quarryman which was to bring him to much wider notice. The quarryman never knew the part he played in Lloyd George's life, as he was dead when his case came to court. The quarryman was a nonconformist, and he had expressed the

wish that his last resting place should be at the side of his
daughter. She happened to be buried in a graveyard belonging
to the Church of England, and the Vicar, showing a surprising
lack of both sympathy and sense, announced that the old man
could be buried in the cemetery, but only in the part reserved for
suicides and people who died without anyone being able to
identify them.

The nonconformists, inevitably, were outraged, and Lloyd
George shared the general indignation. Prompted by his sense of
injustice, he went into the matter in his typically thorough way.
Having done so, he announced his findings. The law of the
land allowed, he claimed, that the quarryman could be buried
by the side of his daughter. He was so confident of the rightness
of his conclusion that he said to his clients, "Take the coffin in
by force if necessary. If the churchyard gates are locked against
you, break them down". And that is just what they did. It
was now the turn of the church authorities to be scandalized.
This was sacrilege and trespass and could not be tolerated.
Legal action was taken and the case was heard in the County
Court before a judge and jury. The jury, reacting to Lloyd
George's eloquence and presentation of his brief, returned a
verdict in favour of the villagers. The judge, however, claimed
that the young solicitor was mistaken on a point of law and gave
judgement for the Church authorities. Lloyd George by no
means discouraged, and confident in his own researches,
promptly appealed to the Lord Chief Justice. And he won his
case.

The matter had been one to excite the attention of all Wales,
and it had also commanded no little attention in England. His
determination and his victory assured his future as a lawyer.
His handling of the affair also served to draw attention to two
qualities in Lloyd George's make-up. The first was his devotion
to detail He exhausted all the material, dealt with every single
item, before preparing his brief. The case also made known his
outspoken disposition. In the years that followed the world was
to come to know the ' Wizard of Wales ' by these qualities, as
well as by several others.

As a boy he had paid at least one visit to the House of
Commons. He was by no means impressed by what he saw

there, as he recorded in his diary. He wrote, "Very much disappointed . . . I will not say I eyed the assembly in the spirit in which William the Conqueror eyed England on his visit to Edward the Confessor—as a region of his future domain".

From his early days he established himself as quick witted and as a brilliant orator and debater. He made many appearances on public platforms. A radical like his uncle, he devoted his energies and eloquence to all matters of reform in his native country, and he was greatly concerned about the unequal position of the poor, the disestablishment of the Church, which provoked a bitter campaign, and about a form of Home Rule for Wales.

Inevitably, because of his temperament and his gifts, he turned to politics. In 1888 he was adopted as Liberal candidate for Caernarvon Borough. A widely sought after speaker, he could arouse the opposite passions of hatred and devotion, and he always retained the interest of his audience. His compatriots rallied round him even as their forefathers had given their support to Owen Glendower. He did not hesitate to carry the attack to that class from which his political opponents were drawn. He chided them without mercy, and his wounding thrusts touched the nerves of his hearers. He had a special technique with hecklers, allowing them to have their say and then cutting them down mercilessly.

On one occasion he asked his audience rhetorically, "What do my opponents want ?" A husky voice replied, "What I want is a change of Government". "No", replied Lloyd George, "What you want is a change of drink !"

One of his most famous remarks was provoked when he was addressing a large meeting and proclaimed, "We must give home rule, not only to Ireland, but to Scotland and also to Wales".

"And home rule for hell !" a heckler shouted.

"Quite right", retorted Lloyd George. "Let every man stick up for his own country !"

Perhaps the retort which he himself would have regarded as his happiest and most effective concerned a speech which he began with the opening words, "I am here". Before he could continue a voice from the back of the hall cried, "And I am here, as well". "Yes", Lloyd George replied, "but you are not all there !"

He was very shrewd and never underrated his opponents. On the contrary, despite his full life, he found time to attend the meetings of his political rivals that he might learn what they were saying. He used the information to excellent purpose at his own public meetings.

In 1888 he married Maggie Owen, a pretty Welsh girl who lived near his own village. In all the varying fortunes of his life she proved to be a true and faithful companion.

He was now the Liberal candidate for the constituency of Caernarvon, and in the two years leading up to the election, he addressed meetings all over North Wales. His Conservative opponent in the election was none other than the squire of his native village, to whom, as a lad, he had been compelled to touch his cap. The old world and the new were set for a head-on collision. But the Conservative candidate and his supporters were not at all disturbed. They regarded the seat as already decided in their favour. But Lloyd George was not the type to concede defeat without fighting with all his resources. It seemed a hopeless contest for him, but he threw himself into it with that immense energy and vitality which were so characteristic of his whole life. The result was a close thing indeed. There were two recounts before he was finally declared the newly and duly elected Member of Parliament for Caernarvon District Boroughs. He had only just done it, but done it he had—by eighteen votes over his opponent. And so, on April 11th, 1890, Parliament acquired one of her most illustrious members.

He continued to represent the constituency until, not long before his death, in 1945, he became Earl Lloyd George of Dwyfor.

When he entered the House of Commons as ' the boy politician ', many people predicted that the eloquent young demagogue would now meet his match and soon be a spent force. But two people did not share this view. One of these, of course, was Lloyd George himself. And the other was his wife, who appreciated his steely resolution and who knew that he regarded this step as the first in his new and true career.

His first task was to study and master the procedure of the House of Commons, while he also assessed the qualities of the famous personages whom, until now, he had never met in person. He readily absorbed the atmosphere and was quick to adapt himself to this new audience, which was as critical as it was intelligent. He soon made the House aware that he had interesting and challenging ideas, bold thoughts and had mastery of the apt and pungent phrase. The Commons began to listen to him with ever increasing attention.

Gladstone was the leader of the Liberal Government, and, nominally, Lloyd George was one of his followers. But it was not in his nature to serve as an echo to anyone, and he was soon seen to be one of the Government's most tireless opponents in individual matters. He had no hesitation in tackling the Grand Old Man, and he treated his successor, Lord Roseberry, in the same cavalier manner. Lloyd George could never be cowed.

In 1894 the Liberals were turned out of office, being replaced by the Conservatives under Joseph Chamberlain. This offered Lloyd George the ideal situation. With the Liberals in opposition, he was now free to oppose to his heart's content and to the limits of his remarkable oratory. Young and idealistic, the Member for Caernarvon fought Joseph Chamberlain, the man of business and of experience. It was indeed, a gladiatorial struggle, for the two men had much in common as well as in their qualities. Both had fought their way to the top, and each was recognised as a master of debate. For Lloyd George, much more than his personal reputation was at stake. He was driven by a passionate desire to see the lot of the ordinary people—the body from which he himself had sprung—greatly improved. He was in revolt against a society which had such false values that it ignored or disdained people like his uncle.

He loved Wales passionately. He was also a nonconformist at a time when nonconformity was a force rapidly gathering strength. He was outraged that the State Church system of England should be imposed on a nation of nonconformists, for this produced unfortunate social consequences. He was enraged and affronted by a system that gave power to the wealthy at the expense of the common people. Regardless of the consequences to himself, he fought for what he believed in. In so doing he gained the respect, though not the affection, of his opponents. In Wales he had acquired national stature.

When the Boer War broke out it was almost inevitable that he should find himself bitterly opposed to it. He saw the hostilities as a powerful nation like Britain attempting to crush a tiny pastoral people, and he found himself likening the South African farmers to the people of Wales. He did not hesitate to speak against the war, and in doing so he earned for himself considerable unpopularity. In spite of this, he was re-elected to his constituency while the Boer War was still in progress.

The General Election of 1905 saw a reversal in the nation's political fortunes. This time the Conservatives were expelled from office, and the Liberals were returned to power with a strong majority. They also had the goodwill of some thirty Labour members. Lloyd George had established himself as a man destined for high office. He combined great skill in debate with a profound respect for facts. On 11th December, 1905, after fifteen years on the back benches pursuing his own course, the Welshman from Llanystumdwy took his seat on the Treasury Bench as President of the Board of Trade. The man who had insisted on remaining a freelance and giving unrestrained voice to his own opinions, was now a member of the Government. The poacher had turned gamekeeper. Lloyd George was now a statesman, and he was to be recognised as such the world over.

There followed a long and successful career. During the forty years or so during which he was to be seen on the political stage, he remained faithful to and fought for his original political beliefs, never losing the love of his native land nor of its people. When he needed to think out his great policies or needed to rest from the exhaustion imposed by his work, it was always to the home on the banks of the River Dwyfor that he returned. He was ever conscious of ' the pit from which he had been dug '. When he was made Chancellor of the Exchequer, with the privilege of residing at No. 11, Downing Street, his first reaction was to observe : "My dear old uncle will be proud to come and stay at the house in which Gladstone, his great hero, at one time lived".

He held all the highest offices open to a Commoner. President of the Board of Trade, Chancellor of the Exchequer, Minister of Munitions, Prime Minister and War Leader and a much-loved Elder Statesman. Yet these exalted positions never caused him to forget his overriding purpose—that of improving the lot of the ordinary people. His achievements in this field had their inspiration in the hard school of his Welsh upbringing and they were carried through because of his superb intelligence, wit and drive. His ' People's Budget ' and his famous Limehouse Speech of 1909 marked the end of an epoch in British history. The social measures which he added to the Statute Book were of immense importance to the people of Wales.

He brought about the Disestablishment of the Welsh Church, and he could claim the major credit for the raising of the school leaving age. Due to his efforts, conditions in the mines were improved, and the triune industries of agriculture, forestry and fisheries were greatly stimulated. He gave an impetus to land reclamation, to the encouragement of rural industries and to road development, all matters vital to the economy of Wales.

My personal experience of Lloyd George, alas, was virtually nil, but my uncle served under him in the Ministry of Munitions. Until then, my uncle had led the sheltered life of a don at Oxford, and he often used to refer to the exhilarating experience of working under ' the little Welshman '. Lloyd George had the deeprooted Welsh reverence for education. He had soon gathered about him a very able staff. A tireless worker himself, he drew out of people reserves of energy they had never suspected they possessed. His powers of persuasion were of the highest order, and his eloquence had to be heard to be believed.

Nevertheless, like all great men—and perhaps like men of every kind—he was far from consistent. He was careless to an embarrassing extent about his personal affairs. The job came first. Friends who required a written answer to a question were fortunate indeed if they received one. Many found it helped to enclose two self-addressed postcards with their enquiries, one marked ' Yes ' and the other marked ' No '. Even with this kind of help, it often happened that Lloyd George failed to send the needed reply. Everyone was aware of his inexhaustible energy and drive. Nevertheless, those who knew him intimately were often baffled and frustrated by what appeared to be spells of laziness. There were times when he seemed to be the victim of a fatal bent for procrastination.

He was quite unable to sit in his office for any length of time. He enjoyed himself far more travelling up and down the country, enlivening the journey by singing Welsh songs. A very stern taskmaster, who expected those under him to give all they had, he was also the kindest and thoughtful of men, and this came very much to the surface when he was dealing with subordinates. His first passion was people, and he showed a particular interest in the young. Although he always had an excessively crowded schedule, he would give the impression that he had all the time in the world—and also the desire—to listen to the other person's point of view.

He had a lively sense of humour and no time at all for convention and pomposity. His favourite reading was historical romance, with a predilection for Dumas. Indeed, one is tempted to wonder whether he did not model himself on D'Artagnon. But his reading was vast and catholic, and he had a tenacious memory, as many found to their cost when they crossed swords with him in debate. He had a vivid imagination and the ability to see into the minds and hearts of other people.

He created quite a problem for his civil servants and secretaries, although almost all of them adored him. His methods were such that they raised certain difficulties in the smooth running of an office. He never prepared a speech beforehand, being so conversant with his subject he could speak on it lengthily, weightily and wittily without the tedium of writing out what he intended to say. He had no sense of timing for his appointments, a weakness which caused his secretaries and agents, as well as party officials no little concern. And he insisted on completing the day's work, no matter how late he and others had to work to do so.

The one who christened Lloyd George the 'Welsh Wizard' was being more than alliterative. He was describing one of the truly great men of the Principality. It was not his friends only who made extravagant claims for him. His rivals and enemies said that he seemed to be gifted with supernatural powers. He certainly deserves his place as one of the great heroes of Wales. His greatest and most enduring memorial is the improvement in the social conditions of the poor, the people he championed.

He died on March 26th, 1945, shortly after being created Earl Lloyd George of Dwyfor. He is buried on the banks of the River Dwyfor, where he used to play as a boy and where he found rest and restoration as a man. His life-long friend, Winston Churchill, one of the few privileged to address him as David, paid him fitting and shining tribute in the House of Commons on the day that his life's work was recalled. He said :

' As a man of action, resource and creative energy he stood, when at his zenith, without a rival. His name is a household word throughout our Commonwealth of Nations. He was the greatest Welshman which that unconquerable race has produced since the age of the Tudors. Much of his work abides, some of it will grow greatly in the future and those who come after us will find the pillars of his life's toil upstanding, massive and indestructible '.

XX

CARAVANSERAI
SUCH ARE THE PEOPLE OF WALES

THERE are many men of Wales who have gained for themselves international fame and acclaim. There are so many, in fact, that many volumes have been written in a vain effort to do justice to them. And in a book of such small compass as this one, all we can do is make mention of only some of them. But it can be said that there is hardly a field of human endeavour or achievement in which the sons of Wales—as well as quite a number of daughters—have not played a distinguished part.

Artistry and imagination are so integral to the Welsh character that it is difficult to exaggerate the contribution the Welsh have made to the worlds of song and poetry. As early as the sixth century the Welsh language had achieved a highly literary form, and the works of poets like Aneirin were already being recorded. It was, in fact, the first language to be properly set out in the British Isles. By the tenth century a very high proportion of the laity were well educated. In Wales, reading and writing did not remain the preserve of the monastery. Three Welsh writers who had achieved international fame during the Middle Ages were Giraldus, Geoffrey of Monmouth and Walter Mapp, and there were many others. The Bible was translated into Welsh during the reign of the Tudors. This was followed, in 1546, by the printing of the first book in Welsh, seventy years after Caxton had set up his printing press in Westminster. This gave such an impetus to printing that there came a stream of religious literature that, in view of the period, was out of all proportion to the size of the population. These books were not printed in Wales, but in England and on the Continent, but they were in Welsh for the Welsh people only. The first Welsh printing pre s was set up in 1778.

Although Welshmen have always joyed in writing for their own people, many have reached out to the far larger audience who speak English and, after the accession of the Tudors, many Welshmen wrote entirely in English, and thereby enriched its literature. There was Henry Vaughan, the Silurist,* and James Howell whom Charles II made his Historiographer Royal. It is said that Howell had the distinction of being the first author to make a livelihood solely out of literature. Dr. John Donne, who became Dean of St. Paul's and one of the greatest poets of the seventeenth century, was of Welsh descent. It is true that his genius as a poet had to wait a long time for recognition, but, in our own century he had been universally recognised as one of the most original writers of English poetry. Charles Kingsley, some two hundred years later, gained fame as the author of *The Water Babies* and such novels as *Hereward the Wake* and *Westward Ho !* He, too, was of Welsh descent. So was the not quite so famous George Meredith and Mary Webb.

It is said that the genius of Shakespeare owes something to the Celtic strain of his grandmother, Alys. More recently a much larger claim has been made regarding Shakespeare's Welsh connections. A book just published sets out to establish that the plays were really written by John Williams of Conway, who lived from 1582 to 1650. Williams was an infant prodigy and had a distinguished career in England, being successively Dean of Westminster, Keeper of the Great Seal, Bishop of Lincoln and Archbishop of York. He was an associate of Francis Bacon, who has also been credited with writing the plays of Shakespeare and who lived from 1561 to 1628. Williams, it must be admitted, had the background and training needed to write Shakespeare's works. But it must be remembered that Shakespeare, who was born in 1564 and died in 1616, ended his first period in 1594. At that time he had already written poems and the three parts of Henry VI and Richard III, at which time Williams was only twelve years old.

Although Wales may not be able to claim that a Welshman produced Shakespeare's works, it can be said that the country's contribution to literature and the arts in the present century has been remarkable. Two young poets of great promise, Wilfred Owen and Edward Thomas, were killed in the First World War. Dylan Thomas was spared such a fate, but, like Christ-

---

*Belonging to the country of the Silures, ancient inhabitants of the south-eastern part of South Wales.

opher Marlowe, unquestionably one of the greatest of the Elizabethan dramatists, he was destined to die too early. The two poets, in fact, had a great deal in common. Kit Marlowe, who penned the famous line, "Was this the face that launched a thousand ships ?" died in a tavern brawl before he had reached the age of thirty. Dylan Thomas did not die so violently, but, unhappily, he consumed himself, spending his rich human resources with such prodigality that he perished in his fortieth year. But, in his brief life he produced poems and the astonishing creation *Under Milk Wood*, which will live as long as the English language is spoken.

In the sphere of prose as in that of poetry Welshmen have done their country and the world most proudly during the twentieth century. Richard Llewellyn's *How Green Was My Valley* demonstrated that a novel dealing with such a grim environment as the South Wales coalfield in a time of depression can be a best seller. Howard Spring, born in Cardiff, is read throughout the English-speaking world. Charles Morgan based his novel, *Sparkenbroke*, on Llandefaelog, near Brecon.

In the world of the theatre Wales has a remarkable record. One of the greatest names of the English stage is that of Ivor Novello, the author of the song, ' Keep the Home Fires Burning ', penned while he was still a youth in Cardiff, and who was a composer, playwright, actor and several other things, all in superb degree. He was a name to be conjured with for almost thirty incredible years. He was very much in the high tradition of Sarah Siddons, who was born in Brecon in 1755, and who is still remembered as one of the world's greatest tragic actresses. Much nearer to Ivor Novello, both in time and versatility, is Emlyn Williams, who has proved himself as an actor, play-wright, manager and elocutionist. A man of not quite so many parts, but a towering figure for all that is Richard Burton. There are many others who might be mentioned who have made their names in the cinema, the theatre and on television.

Wales, of course, is pre-eminently the Land of Song. So true is this that some eight hundred years ago Gerald of Wales drew attention to the singing to be heard in certain areas of the country. The Welsh choirs have inspired all the great compos-ers, and it is from them that Handel is said to have drawn the theme of the Hallelujah Chorus. The harp is a Celtic adaptation of the ancient lyre, and, at one time, it was so popular it was to be found in every Welsh home, while today it is particularly associated with Wales.

A well-known nineteenth century composer was Dr. Joseph Parry, who was born in Merthyr Tydfil. His famous hymn tune, *Aberystwyth*, was composed on the banks of the River Taff. More famous are two composers of this century. Walford Davies is one of these, and gained the honour of Master of the King's Musick. The organist at St. George's chapel, Windsor, he became the Director of Music and Chairman of the National Council of Music, at the University of Wales, and also the Gresham Professor of Music. He did much to make Welsh music known to a wide audience. Equally famous was Ralph Vaughan Williams, who studied in Berlin under Max Bruch and in Paris under Ravel. He wrote nine symphonies, ballets, chamber music, some very well-known songs, and the two famous operas, ' Hugh the Drover ' and ' Riders to the Sea '.

There has never been a Welsh school of art. In spite of this, the Principality has made important contributions in this sphere. Richard Wilson, who became a member of the Royal Academy, was born at Machynlleth in 1714. He won fame as both a landscape and a portrait painter, ranked as one of the foremost artists of his day and greatly influenced the English school. One of the most famous people to sit for him was Flora Macdonald, who saved the life of Prince Charles Edward after the defeat at Culloden Moor in 1746.

Known the world over is Augustus John, who was particularly noted for his portraits. Among the many famous people he painted were Lloyd George, Bernard Shaw and T. E. Lawrence. Some of his works are to be seen in the Tate Gallery, among them *Galways* and *The Smiling Woman*. Of equal fame as an artist was Sir Frank Brangwyn, who died in 1956. He was regarded as the greatest mural artist and etcher of his day.

In architecture, too, Wales has a proud record. One of the great names in this field is that of Inigo Jones, who became known as ' the English Palladio '. He built many famous structures, amongst them the Banqueting Hall at Whitehall and the gateway of St. Mary's at Oxford. He was a Royalist, and his sympathies cost him dearly in the Civil War. A Welsh architect who planned some of London's most famous places was John Nash, who died in 1835 at the age of eighty-three. He planned Regent Street and laid out Regent's Park. He also enlarged Buckingham Palace and designed the Marble Arch. The people of Brighton have reason to remember him, for it was John Nash who designed their Pavilion.

The pottery and porcelain of Swansea are sought after by all collectors. The factory which made this china-ware was built in 1769 and continued in production until 1870. All over Wales the art of making pottery and earthenware is still being developed.

The oldest Welsh rural craft is the making and using of the coracle. These are still to be seen in West Wales on the rivers Teifi and Towy in spite of the determined efforts of the Fisheries Boards to put an end to them. It was in a coracle that Prince Madoc learnt the skills of seamanship.

Until the 18th century Wales, with a population of 400,000 or so, was almost wholly rural. Inevitably, the economy was rooted in agriculture, and the cattle, sheep and pigs produced in Wales filled the English markets. But from the earliest times Wales had been famous for her mineral resources, and the Tudors had done much to explore and assess them. That is why, when the industrial revolution got under way and roads and canals were developed, Wales underwent a transformation. The country became industrialized. Her huge reserves of coal were of obvious worth, and so were the copper, iron and slate that were to be found beneath her soil. These basic industries resulted in the establishment of subsidiary concerns. There was wealth to be made in Wales, and ever larger amounts of capital flowed into the country from over the border. Into the country, too, came English and Irish workers seeking employment in the expanding economy. Most of them found the work, but not many found the wealth.

Like every other country, Wales suffered from the alternations of boom and slump, dictated by war and by economic factors which no one then really understood. Following upon the Napoleonic Wars came a period of stagnation. In Wales the conditions of the workers were as bad as they were elsewhere.

The Welsh workers knew hardship and near destitution, and they had that independence of spirit which caused them to make known how they felt about their situation. There were the Chartist riots and the Rebecca riots of the 19th century, in which the Welsh gave expression to their passionate concern for justice. One of the legacies of the industrial revolution is to be found in the strength of the Labour and Trade Union movements in Wales.

It is sometimes forgotten that Keir Hardie, who is rightly regarded as the founder of the British Labour Party, and as the one who forged the link between the Party and the Trade Unions, was returned as the Member of Parliament for Merthyr Tydfil in 1900. He retained the seat, with increased majorities in three successive elections until his death in 1915.

It would be false indeed to give the impression that all the employers who made their fortunes in Wales exploited their workers. There were those, like the Guests and the Humphreys, who were enlightened employers and who treated their workers with a sense of justice. They did more. They devoted much of their fortunes to Wales, and they did much to establish the system of industrial apprenticeship and to provide means of education for the workers.

The industrial revolution took the railway to Wales as it took this means of transport to so many countries. And David Davies of Llandinam, the self-made capitalist from Montgomery, built railways all over the Principality. His life spanned those expansive years of 1818 to 1890, and he built railways and a new dock at Barry, and still found time to operate coal fields in the Rhondda Valley. He was seen to be a man of such wide experience and knowledge that he was consulted by foreign governments anxious to expand or establish railways and heavy industries. He represented Cardiganshire as a Liberal, and he was one of the first Governors of University College of Wales. During the second half of the nineteenth century he did much for the cause of education and religion in Wales. In his person he embodied all the principles of the Calvinistic Movement. He believed in hard work and in self-denial, was an uncompromising opponent of drink and a strict Sabbatarian. Although David Davies reflected the virtues of his day, and most of his principles have been discarded in many quarters, teetotalism and Sunday observance are subjects which still provoke lively discussion in Wales. Religion is still held in high esteem in Wales, and, indeed, it is true to say that, whether all human beings are or not, the Welshman is still a religious animal. He is also devoted to education. In some of the western nations education is treated with a certain degree of cynicism. But in Wales it is held in reverence.

The Welsh people enjoyed their religion. It was never something they accepted as a mere formality. Methodism, like several other sects, found fertile soil in Wales, and most Welshmen and women are aware that Charles Wesley wrote his haunting hymn, ' Jesu, lover of my soul ' at Garth, in Breconshire. Nonconformity has acquired a reputation in many countries for its lack of grace and beauties in its buildings and its forms of worship. It must be admitted that many of the Welsh chapels are no better than their English counterparts. But nonconformity in Wales has been saved from ugliness and a soul-chilling dullness by the tradition of music and poetry. The great hymn writers have always had a tremendous influence in the Principality. And because of their love of oratory and poetry, they have been most discriminating sermon tasters and have joyed in great preachers.

It should be remembered that, in the church, it was the Englishman, William Laud, Bishop of St. David's from 1621— 1626, who encouraged Welsh-speaking clergy in his diocese. When he became Archbishop of Canterbury he appointed Welsh-speaking men of Wales to all the Welsh Bishoprics. William Laud, a supporter of Charles I, had the misfortune to be impeached by the Long Parliament and was executed for treason in 1645. But he proved himself to be a true friend of Wales.

The Welsh circulating schools have been recognised as one of the landmarks in the history of education. No less and unlikely a person than Catherine of Russia sent commissioners to study them. They were instituted by Griffith Jones of Llanddowror, Carmarthen. The schools were held in the same places annually and usually in the three winter months when there was but little farm work to be done. Evening schools—commonly referred to as ' night classes '—were provided for those who could not attend during the day. The subjects were, or necessity, limited, the pupils being taught to read the Welsh Bible and to learn the Church catechism. It was Griffith Jones who trained the teachers and wrote most of the text-books for these schools. That he laboured to some purpose is obvious from the fact that, when he died in 1761, there had been set up the huge total of no less than 3,485 schools which, in their twenty-five years, had taught the amazing total of 158,000 pupils. It was an achievement that was to have a lasting effect on education in Wales.

Griffith Jones was a clergyman, and so was Thomas Charles. A native of Bala, Charles had realised the value of the circulating schools and he was determined to provide a substitute. He had been educated at Carmarthen Academy and Jesus College, Oxford, which had always maintained close links with Wales, and he set about the task of training a body of travelling teachers. It was later decided that these schools should meet on Sundays. Thomas Charles was not the founder of the Sunday School Movement, as that achievement is accredited to Robert Raikes. But it was due to Charles's organising ability that these Sunday Schools were placed on a sound foundations. He supervised the preparation of the Bible in Welsh At the outset, he opposed the movement which led to the split between the Anglican Church and the Welsh Calvinistic Movement. But, in 1813, he revised his position and decided to support the establishment of the Welsh Calvinistic Church as a separate body. In fact, he was one of those who drew up the form of ordination which is still used today by the denomination.

One of the makers of modern Wales was undoubtedly Howell Harris, who lived from 1714 to 1773. He well deserved the title of ' the trumpet voiced '. It has been claimed that he was the greatest Welshman of his generation. It is a claim that seems to stand, for he was the embodiment of the Welsh religious rennaissance, that spiritual force which remains so strong in Wales even today. A brilliant preacher, he could, like Owen Glendower before him and Lloyd George after him, play with consummate skill on all the chords of the human heart. He was, too, a hymn writer of considerable power. He chose Trefecca, in Breconshire, as the place in which to establish his ' Family '. The members of this were really his supporters, whom he had brought together in a community. That the family might be self-supporting they raised their own buildings in which they taught and pursued occupations of various kinds. Seminaries were established for the training of evangelists. Howell Harris, in fact, was the pioneer of the rural technological colleges of the present day. It is fitting that the R.T.I. in Breconshire at Penlan should be named after him. Harris proved himself a pioneer in quite a different quarter. He was one of those who, in 1755, founded the Brecknockshire Agricultural Society. This was not only the first of its kind in Wales, but was one of the first in the British Isles.

It would be possible to site many more Welshmen, as well as quite a number of Welsh women, who have made significant contributions to the life of Wales and also to those many peoples who make up the English-speaking world. All we have been able to do here is touch lightly on the wealth of talent which is the heritage of Wales. Judged by any standard her achievements are remarkable. But when it is remembered that her population even today numbers less than 3 million, then what she has achieved is astonishing. There may have been no Golden Age of Wales, but there has been a very long period of the purest silver. The Welsh have shown that there are many princes amongst her people.

XXI

THE FIGHTING MEN OF WALES

' Look you, I will be so bold as to tell you I know the disciplines of war : and there is an end '.
— SHAKESPEARE, *Henry V.*

WALES has a long and distinguished military history, and one of which she is justifiably proud. Surrounded on three sides by the sea, she accepted the challenge of the oceans in her earliest days, and Welsh sailors have served with distinction in the Royal Navy since its formation. Many have also played their part in the highly critical battles and work of the Royal Air Force. But it is, of course, as soldiers that Welshmen played the most prominent part in the bleak and testing business of war.

From earliest times, resistance to the succession of invaders of these islands has hardened in the mountains of the West. On more than one occasion, the intruder has felt that everything was going his way until he encountered the fighting men of Wales. Their enemies, like their friends and neighbours, were compelled again and again to respect their martial qualities.

The Romans, so justly famed for their fighting spirit and abilities, understood well the worth of the Welsh. During their occupation of Britain, they welcomed Welshmen into their ranks. And the Emperor Magnus Maximus paid them one of the many high compliments they were to receive from time to time during the next sixteen hundred years. When he withdrew from Britain with the intention of conquering the north western regions of Europe, he was careful to take a contingent of Welsh Legionnaires with him.

During the Dark Ages it was the Welsh who repelled the Danes and pagan Saxons. Other invaders from the continent fared no better. The Normans established themselves in England without undue difficulty until they found themselves facing the Welsh. Then they discovered that they were dealing with an unusually tough and devious enemy. The Welsh had geographical advantages lacking to the English, but it must be recorded that they made the most of them. The men of Wales made the fullest use of their forests and mountain fastnesses by resorting to guerilla tactics which repeatedly frustrated the Normans and caused them considerable losses.

The development of the longbow during the twelfth century marked a climacteric in the history of warfare. It proved as revolutionary as the introduction of the repeating rifle and machine-gun were to be hundreds of years later. It was a Welsh invention, and the Welsh archer was recognised as the one able to make superlative use of the weapon. For several centuries it dominated the battlefields of Europe, for whoever had mastery with the longbow was more than likely to emerge as the victor in warfare.

Edward I was one of the first to recognise the value of the new weapon. He saw to it that a contingent of Welsh bowmen fought in his army against the Scots. And they played no small part in achieving the defeat of Wallace and the submission of Robert Bruce. Edward III had reason to be grateful to the Welsh bowmen. It was they who assured him his victory over the French at Crecy in 1346. It is said that no less than 5,000 Welshmen took part in that battle. Ten years later, the Welsh put the Black Prince in their debt again at the Battle of Poitiers.

Welsh mercenaries were always welcomed into the ranks of the Free Companies, the bodies immortalized by Sir Arthur Conan Doyle in *The White Company* and other stories. They were not only distinguished for their skill as archers. They were recognised as possessed of rare physical courage and endurance, and famed for their ability to march long distances. The Welsh infantry have the same reputation even today.

There were some Welshmen who so joyed in warfare that it seems that almost anybody's fight was theirs, too. One of Wales's most distinguished soldiers of fortune was Owain de Galles, who fought with a band of Welshmen for the French against Edward III. In this lengthy quarrel, men from Wales were to be found on both sides. It was another Owen, in this case Owen Glendower, who was so well served by his compatriots. They also played an honourable part in the victory of the English King at Agincourt.

Shakespeare left a most apt and admirable word picture of Welsh soldiers, describing them as tough, argumentative and full of humour. They are, as experience has taught me, exactly like that today.

We have already seen the vital part they played both in the Wars of the Roses and in the Civil Wars of the 17th century. But that is only a fraction of their story. Lord Hopton, the Royalist in Cornwall, in 1645 had in his ranks 400 Welshmen. On the 1st March that year, it is on record that they all got drunk, "It being Taffy's Day". St. David's Day was as much a day of celebration as it is today.

In the Irish Rebellion at the end of the 18th century Sir Watkin William Wynn led a force of Welsh cavalry against those in revolt. They were naturally not much loved by the Irish for their pains, and they were given the name of ' The Bloody Britons '. It seems fair to conclude that Napoleon Bonaparte felt pretty much the same way about Welsh fighters. He had good reason to detest the Pembroke Yeomanry, for it was this body who, in 1797, joined forces with that astonishing woman, Jemima Nicholas, and her Amazons. They not only frustrated Napoleon's plans, but they also succeeded in wiping out the Black Legion. Fishguard is a much prized battle honour.

The British Army as we know it today came into existence after the restoration of King Charles. Its emergence as a newly constituted fighting force was made possible by the extinction of feudal tenure. In the three hundred or so years which have elapsed since then there is hardly a single important campaign fought by the British Army in which the soldiers of Wales have not played a glorious, sometimes decisive, part. They have been represented in every branch of the Army, but it is in the vital field of the infantry that their main contribution has been made.

In the many churches and memorials to be seen throughout Wales is evidence of the sacrifices men of Wales have made in every corner of the world. Space prevents any treatment in detail of the numerous campaigns—recorded in the regimental colours—which tell the story of the two great nations in arms. There are four Welsh Regiments in the British Army. In the order in which they came into existence, they are The Royal

Welch Fusiliers, 23rd Regiment of foot, established in 1689 ; The South Wales Borderers Regiment, established in the same year ; the 41st and 69th which now make up the Welch Regiment, formed in 1714, and the Welsh Guards, which form part of the Brigade of Guards, and which came into existence in 1915.

The Colonel of the 24th was no less a person than John Churchill, Duke of Marlborough. In the battles and campaign of the Wars of the Spanish Succession, he had under his command both the Royal Welch Fusiliers and The South Wales Borderers. Both regiments carry the battle honours of Marlborough's four great victories—Blenheim (1704), Ramillies (1706), Oudenarde (1708), and Malplaquet, which completed the brilliant quartet in 1709. The Royal Welch Fusiliers were with George II in 1743 when he defeated the French at Dettingen, on the last occasion in which a British monarch led his forces in the field.

The Welsh infantry have not only distinguished themselves on land. Before war achieved its modern highly specialised form it was the custom for infantry to carry out the duties now undertaken by the Royal Marines. In those days it was the infantry who were attached to naval vessels and who had the duty of storming ashore. Which explains why the 69th Regiment served under Horatio Nelson when he commanded H.M.S. *Agamemnon* as a Captain. Later they served under him on H.M.S. *Captain* as the Battle of Cape St. Vincent, in 1797. He always greeted them affectionately as, "My old Agamemnons". The Welch Regiment cherishes Nelson's memory, and not only by celebrating Trafalgar Day. They are proud of the unique honour of the Naval Crown which graces their regimental colour.

All the regiments of Wales served with distinction in the Peninsular War under Sir John Moore and Wellington, who defeated the French when they fought against him under their brilliant and brave commander, Marshal Soult. They played their part in defeating Napoleon at Waterloo at the beginning of the nineteenth century, and continued throughout the whole of the Victorian era, appearing in a series of wars which took place in almost a'l parts of the world. The battle honours show the part played by the Welsh regiments. They fought on every continent and in every war, proving themselves then, as now, as able and worthy ambassadors as Britain can produce.

In this strife-ridden twentieth century they have, inevitably, been busier than ever. They have seen service in the South African War, the First and Second World Wars, in Korea, Palestine, Malaya, Cyprus and Aden. They are today part of the Army of the Rhine, playing their part in the many peace-keeping roles which have always gained for the British soldier the highest praise, except from those whose peace they were keeping, often at much cost to themselves. It is not always appreciated that, during the Great War of 1914—1918, in addition to serving in the Royal Navy and other branches of the Army, and in addition to furnishing the sinews of war, the men of Wales produced no less than ninety-six battalions. Their contribution, judged by any standard, was beyond all praise.

One of these battalions was the history-making Welsh Guards. On 26th of February, 1915, King George V authorised the formation of a Regiment of Foot Guards of Wales. It was in that same year, appropriately, on St. David's Day, that the regiment first mounted guard at Buckingham Palace. Since then, they have added to the roll of honours won by the men of Wales.

The Regiments of Wales are an integral part of the life of the Principality. Almost every family in the country can claim a relative or friend who has served or is serving in one of the Welsh Regiments. Their shop windows are depots, headquarters and regimental museums, and a very active and flourishing Old Comrades Association keep alive this comradely spirit in every town and district. Great pride is taken in the achievements of 'The Regiment' both on duty and in sport, and particularly in Rugby Football, a game in which they all four excel.

Each regiment has its own distinctive dress. On the left of their bearskins the Welsh Guards wear a plume that is green at the centre flanked by white. Their tunic buttons are arranged in groups of five to denote their place in the hierarchy of the Household Division. The Leek is attached to the cap that is worn with the service dress. The Royal Welch Fusiliers are readily identified by the black flash which hangs down the back of the collar. This is a relic of the eighteenth century bow of the pigtail which this Regiment was the last to wear. The badge of the bursting grenade denotes their role as Fusiliers. The South Wales Borderers wear a cap badge of the Sphinx of Egypt surrounded by a silver wreath of immortelles. The Sphinx has considerable significance. It is a reminder of the part the Borderers played in 1801 in the fight against the French. The Wreath also evokes memories. It was awarded by Queen Victoria in recognition of the gallantry shown in the Zulu Wars which saved Natal from massacre. The defence of Rorke's Drift in 1879 is too well known to require repeating here. It is recalled annually as a great regimental occasion. Men of the Welch Regiment display the Plume of Feathers of the Prince of Wales, and the collar is a replica of the Welsh Dragon. All the isignia of the four Regiments of Wales are arresting and evocative. They are worn with pride, for they have been earned by courage and prowess in the exacting sphere of mortal combat.

Before the Battle of Waterloo was joined, the Duke of Wellington was asked what he thought of his chances of victory. He pointed to a private of the infantry and observed that the outcome of the engagement lay in his hands. And he spoke prophetically. Napoleon was, in fact, defeated by the infantry men who, stout of heart, refused to accept defeat.

Today, the cry is for economy, and the needs of the Welfare State are regarded as of more importance than the needs of national defence and influence overseas. It has been decided that cuts must be made in the armed services. As always and, in my opinion, unwisely, the axe is to fall on the infantry, the arm which, as Field Marshal Earl Wavell said, "Wins all the battles and all the wars". The Regiments of Wales are to be greatly reduced. When the pruning is finished only the Welsh Guards and two regular battalions forming the Welsh Brigade* will remain. The Brigade is part of the Prince of Wales's Division. History plays peculiar tricks, and it has certainly

---

*In the most recent reorganisation the Welsh Brigade will consist of the Royal Welch Fusiliers and the Royal Regiment of Wales.

done so here. The bowler hat brigade of Whitehall have made a happy choice in deciding that Lichfield is to serve as the Headquarters of this Division. It was in the spot where Lichfield stands that King Offa planned the Dyke that he saw would make his position secure on the Welsh border !

George II had good reason to be grateful to the Welch Fusiliers for their exploits in the Battle of Dettingen in 1744. And he showed his gratitude by conferring on them the White Horse of Hanover and the motto that is so charged with pride, "Nor do hardships dismay". There could hardly be a more fitting motto for the fighting men of Wales. Great regiments are rooted in great traditions and the family spirit. The Regiments of Wales have both to a marked degree. Nor, happily, will reorganisation impair the greatness. The Welsh soldier will continue to show that he is inspired by the same high courage that informed his forbears at Crecy and Agincourt. In peace and war he will maintain the admirable tradition that Wales has forged.

Postscript

The South Wales Borderers and the Welch Regiment will form the Royal Regiment of Wales whose Colonel in Chief is H.R.H. Prince Charles. The Royal Regiment of Wales and the Royal Welch Fusiliers will form the Welsh Brigade.

EPILOGUE

WALES TODAY

ALL nations are proud of their history, and almost all have reason for their pride. Few peoples which have figured significantly in man's tremendous and baffling story, whether ancient or medieval or modern, have been without their courage, their own peculiar and admirable traits, and, of course, their great men.

The people of Wales are aware of this. In making claims for themselves, they know that other nations have reason to raise their heads and to point proudly to their past. Even so, the Welsh story, as we have seen, has some near-to-unique features. Few nations have excelled to such a high degree in both the arts of war and peace. And so many peoples lacking independence have either spent all their moral and intellectual resources striving—often in vain—to gain their freedom, or they have felt too oppressed or absorbed or affronted to assert themselves in the arts or the sciences or in civilization.

The Welsh, like the Scots, have not fallen into any of these traps. While prizing liberty and independence as highly as the breath of life itself, they have asserted themselves over the centuries, making significant contributions to arts and letters, to government and politics, to science and education. And the present in no way lags behind the past.

I find it a sombre thought that the children who came into the world in the year that I came to live in Brecon have now left school. In these swift, brief years I have seen many changes in Wales, changes which would have delighted the hearts of the Princes who have featured in this book. In every field, the development of the Principality as the equal partner of England, Scotland and Northern Ireland has been immense. And Wales has made this progress without losing so much as one degree of her own peculiar genius and individuality.

In the sphere of government there has been something of a revolution during the last decade. In 1958 Wales was given more realistic recognition when Westminster created the office of Minister of State for Welsh Affairs. There was a further advance in 1964, when the Right Honourable James Griffiths, c.h., m.p., to whom I am indebted for the Foreword to this work, was appointed Her Majesty's Secretary of State for Wales with cabinet rank.

The Welsh office was established in Cardiff, and, in 1955, this town was raised to the status of the capital city of Wales. But the process continues, and with considerable momentum. It is proposed to reorganise the Government in Wales. When this happens, the administration may revert to the ancient divisions of the land, and also a Council of Wales may be brought into being. This may not only prove the prelude to a further devolution of Government from Westminster, but the change will take place on the lines advocated by none other than Llywelyn the Great some seven hundred and fifty years ago.

The wisdom of the Welsh, however, is to be seen in what is happening in their country at the present time. A people of considerable resource are making more and more of their natural resources. All the time there is going on a steady expansion of agriculture and forestry, which in the short term, and even more so in the long term, are of such value to the national economy. Famous throughout the world are the Welsh bred Hereford cattle. So, too, are the powerfully built Welsh Blacks. In the old pre-transport days, Welsh Blacks were known to be so strong that they were shod and driven across Wales and England to the Smithfield market.

The hill farmers of Wales make nonsense of the theory that the small farm is no longer economically visible. The sheep farmers in the Snowdon range meet with many difficulties, but they show themselves to be successful with their stock. Run by families mainly, these holdings are of considerable value to the country.

It was not land, but minerals which attracted the early settlers to Wales, and today the biggest steel works in Europe are situated in the Principality. The coal fields stretch from Monmouthshire to East Carmarthenshire. Milford Haven, chosen by Henry Tudor for his landing in 1485, has been developed into one of the world's major oil ports, while, even now, a huge nuclear power station is being built in North Wales.

It has been decided to transfer the Royal Mint to the Principality, and, all the time, firms of international fame are moving into the country. Wales, in fact, is now experiencing another industrial revolution. The pressure on territory is now such that it has been decided to set up a panel to deal with derelict land.

The development of rural electricity, the telephone and the improvement of the roads have played their part in bringing the Welsh villages into the general stream of progress.

A glance at the budget of the County Councils indicates the high esteem in which education is held in the Celtic heart. This is in the tradition of Owen Glendower. Though dead more than five hundred and fifty years, he would indeed rejoice could he see the continued expansion of the University of Wales and the growth of adult education that is taking place all over the Principality.

There is, however, a shadow over the country. In the pursuit of progress water has become a vital issue for an expanding population and a rapidly developing industry. In the past, rural Wales has given generously of her reserves, supplying the needs of its own urban communities and such major cities as Liverpool and Birmingham. The planners are now casting covetous eyes on the valleys of Wales, those valleys which are rich in the produce vital to a nation which has to import much of its food. But a halt must be called, for the obvious solution is by no means the best one. Agricultural land will have to be lost for buildings of various kinds and for roads. But surely, in this day of technology, our scientists can make available, at reasonable cost, all the water that is needed, without draining the Welsh valleys. Surely the Treasury can find sufficient money for the necessary research to discover the desalination of sea water in ways that are sufficiently economical. This would do more than solve the water problem for the foreseeable future. It would preserve for many generations still to come the great historical heritage of Wales.

That heritage is evident on every hand. The industrial belt is bounded by the Brecon Beacons National Park to the north and by the fertile and beautiful sea coast to the south. The worker is never far from the beauties of nature. North and mid-Wales, with their ever changing landscape of the ranges of

Snowdonia and the Cambrian mountains, complement the hidden valleys, the moors and estuaries which have remained unchanged over the centuries and which still offer escape and shelter from the stresses of present-day living.

Perhaps the battle of the Welsh countryside will be won on the playing fields of the Principality. There could be no more fitting place for such a victory. And it is one that the Welsh people must not lose. For, in a world growing weary of artificial playgrounds, Wales has the natural beauty that is being more and more highly prized. In the sea that washes her shores, in the inland waters, the mountains and forests, there is a magnificence beyond price. And there is, too, excellent fishing and first-rate shooting. Another attraction is Welsh hospitality, which cannot be bettered anywhere in the world. The Wales Tourist Board is active in making Wales known to the world, and she has in this an economic asset to complement her expanding industries.

Recently, I attended the ceremony of the enthronement of the Lord Archbishop and Metropolitan of the Province of Wales. Colourful and impressive, the occasion recalled for me the valiant struggles of Giraldus and Lloyd George who fought with such determination to gain the independence of the Welsh Church.

The investiture of His Royal Highness, Prince Charles, will be just as significant for Wales as that initial enactment which took place in 1301. It will be marked by all the pageantry and music which the Welsh rightly regard as so precious. It would, I feel, be fitting if the occasion were marked in a manner the Welsh would find most pleasing. Lord Melbourne once remarked that he liked the Order of the Garter because there was ' no damn'd merit about it '. He spoke in jest, of course, but the Garter, like the Thistle and St. Patrick, is rather individual and national. It has always surprised me that Wales has never had its own Order of Chivalry. I feel it would be fitting if consideration were given to something on the lines of the Most Excellent Order of the British Empire. I would like to see instituted an Order of the Principality of Wales, with perhaps certain grades. The Order would be conferred on those who have brought distinction to the Principality, or who had rendered valuable service to its people. The badge would naturally be the Welsh Dragon and the ribbon would be of the national colours. Wales deserves this type of recognition, and it would be appropriate to found such an Order in the year of Prince Charles's investiture.

A majestic achievement that has not yet been mentioned is the Severn Bridge—surely one of the wonders of the modern world. It has done much to forge the links between the peoples of Wales and England. Whatever degree of independence the Welsh people achieve, and it is bound to increase and develop, there will always be a close bond of union between Wales and England. John Milton, one of the great Englishmen, was at Ludlow Castle, which for many generations served as the seat of Government for the Welsh Marches, when he wrote his masque, ' Comus ', for the induction of the Lord President of the Council for Wales. Four of his lines provide a fitting ending for our work :

> ' And all this tract that fronts the falling sun,
> A noble peer of mickle trust and power,
> Has in his charge, with temper'd awe to guide
> An old, and haughty nation proud in arms '.

ENVOI

' Let no man despise Wales, her language and her literature. She has survived many storms, she has survived many Empires. Her time will come. When the last truck load of coal reaches Cardiff, when the last black diamond is dug out of the earth of Glamorgan, there will be men then digging gems of pure brilliance from the mines of the literature and language of Wales '.

DAVID LLOYD GEORGE.

St. David's Day, 1906.

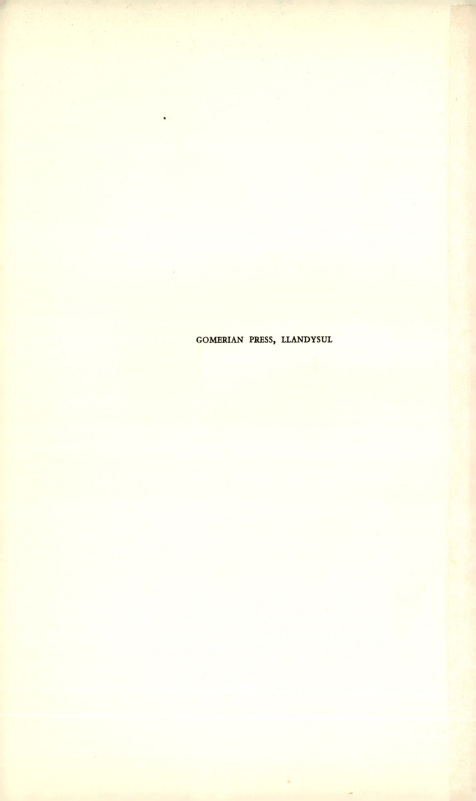

GOMERIAN PRESS, LLANDYSUL